MODERN PUBLIC AFFAIRS PROGRAMMING

Other TAB books by the author:

No. 819 *Journalist's Notebook of Live Radio-TV News*

No. 977
$14.95

MODERN PUBLIC AFFAIRS PROGRAMMING

BY PHILLIP KEIRSTEAD

TAB BOOKS
BLUE RIDGE SUMMIT, PA. 17214

FIRST EDITION

FIRST PRINTING—FEBRUARY 1979

Copyright © 1979 by TAB BOOKS

Printed in the United States of America

Library of Congress Cataloging in Publication Data

Keirstead, Phillip O.
  Modern public affairs programming.

  Includes index.
  1. Radio programs, Public service. 2. Television programs, Public service. 3. Broadcasting—United States. I. Title.
PN1990.9.P82K4   791.44'5   78-12942
ISBN 0-8306-8977-X

Contents

Preface

The public affairs share of broadcasting is growing. Typically, in the large, highly structured stations, it has become an activity of and by itself with its own managing vice-president. But at a majority of stations, public affairs programming is still a hodgepodge of shared duties and responsibilities. Hopefully, this book will encourage more station managers to sort out public affairs functions and assign someone the task of giving their public affairs programming direction and organization.

The author believes in writing very practical books. Much of what is contained herein is in the words of the practitioners—the managers, public affairs directors, editorial directors. It is written to be read by others who have these responsibilities, as an aid in their planning. It is also written for students and their professors; they share the responsibility of molding the future of broadcasting in this country.

Before we embark, a word of thanks to the many broadcasters who willingly gave of their time to be interviewed, to correspond and to share years of experience—perhaps the most valuable resource we have.

Another word of thanks goes to the many public affairs experts in industry, non-profit organizations and government who have been most helpful. Special mention goes to Ben Futterfield of the National Park Service who has been a source of much sage advice.

The last—and most important—word of thanks goes to Sonia-Kay Keirstead, who has endured the agonies which accompanied this task, and who lent advice, encouragement and just plain hard work when all were most needed. Thanks!

Phillip O. Keirstead

About the Author

Phillip O. Keirstead is an associate professor of journalism at Florida Agricultural and Mechanical University.

In the fields of journalism, broadcasting, and radio-TV news, Keirstead is a widely read and highly respected writer.

Chapter 1
Introduction

This book was written to be read by two groups—broadcasters, including students and teachers, and people who seek exposure by using free broadcast time for their ideas and organizations.

We will use the term "public affairs" as a blanket, covering any activity which informs and enlightens the community, other than spot, hard news coverage. These activities include programs, editorials, documentaries and mini-documentaries.

Our major concentration will be on programs, rather than brief announcements known as public service spots. At some points we will talk about the purely external, non-broadcast activities of a station in its community.

To us, it doesn't matter whether or not the program is sponsored. We are interested in the service it provides to the community.

We will take particular note of editorials and the utilization of the right to reply to editorials. We will also be concerned with the twistings and turnings of the rules governing political broadcasts.

We will pay attention to the process—called ascertainment— by which stations attempt to define the public affairs needs of their community.

You will find that our definition of public affairs broadcasts will run the gamut from a sponsored audience call-in program on a small community station in Maine, to a sophisticated documentary series done by a network-owned giant in New York City.

The important point to us is to do the best we can with existing resources. With this in mind, we will provide a number of basic ideas which can be adapted to many different types of markets.

WHY STATIONS DO PUBLIC AFFAIRS

Broadcast stations do public affairs programming because they have to! Broadcasting in the United States is a franchise granted by the government. The federal government accepts applications from interested parties and parcels out franchises to operate in defined areas with defined facilities on exclusive frequencies.

You cannot legally set up a radio or television transmitter (on the customary bands) and begin broadcasting just because the idea strikes your fancy. You must have the permission of the Federal Communications Commission.

The Federal Communications Commission (FCC) provides order through regulation of the airwaves, so that they are not filled with an endless cacaphony of clashing signals.

Since there are usually many more applicants than there are frequencies available, the FCC has the unenviable task of deciding who will be granted the franchise to use a certain frequency in a specific locality. How does the FCC make these determinations? — by deciding how well each station provides certain services to its community.

The FCC does not have the authority to tell a broadcaster what *specific* programs to air, but the Commission does have the authority to outline certain broad objectives to be accomplished as a means of measuring the quality of the station's services to its community.

These services include opportunities for various political, ethnic, religious, civic and educational groups to discuss their ideas, plans, objectives, etc. on the air. The FCC demands that each time the station seeks to renew its license, it state some general plans and quantities of time that it will set aside for these broad, public service programming categories.

A parallel concept, grown out of this process of qualitative and quantitative appraisal, is localism. The FCC gives greater weight to programs which are originated locally and which involve the local community—the theory being that the local broadcaster can judge the needs of the community best and can tailor programming to meet those needs.

Thus it looks with greater favor on a station which airs three locally-originated religious programs a week, than one which picks up two religious programs from out-of-town organizations and gets a third from its network.

Much of this programming falls generally in a category we call "public affairs." To some, the term public affairs means a dull news interview type of program. Actually, public affairs programming can be interesting and commercially successful, if sufficient thought and creativity are applied to the task. Even though broadcast stations do public affairs programs because the FCC tells them they have to, it's also a matter of enlightened self-interest. Community involvement, getting talked about around town, getting your name (call letters or channel) remembered, they're all vital to the success of a broadcast station. That's reason enough to be serious about doing public affairs programming.

Then there's the theory of participation in government. Early in our history our forefathers established the concept of citizen participation, of universal education. The success of our way of living, of governing, depends on an enlightened populace. We of the mass media have an important role to play in opening the channels of communication—in stimulating discussion of the issues which are important in our nation and our communities. These are the final, and most important reasons we do public affairs programs!

Community Image

One of the most important long-term investments a television or radio station can make is to establish the sort of "image" it wishes to convey to its community. Most farsighted managers want their station to be thought of as "the station"…an integral part of the communities they serve. Image means audience loyalty and sales dollars.

In addition, a station which truly convinces its audience that it is part of the community will have far less difficulty in making a convincing case at renewal time, or, if need be, when it is called upon to fight off a competing application!

Most experienced broadcasters will tell you that image—the public's impression of a station—has important effects at all levels. For example, an account executive goes out to sell commercial time on a popular music radio station. The potential advertiser may say, depending on his tastes, "all you people do is play music for kids." The station manager has to decide if this is the image he wishes to perpetuate. If the station wants to trade on a loyal following of youthful listeners, then it is accomplishing its objective, and has the image it desires. But, if the station wishes to be the center for information in the community, then it has failed.

The ideal position to be in is to be able to say: "Look, we serve this community, we're here, we understand your problems a whole lot better than some station over there."

To accomplish this sort of image, a station must have a good two-way relationship with its community. It must serve its audience, and must involve the audience in the station.

Ward Quaal and James Brown, in their book on *Broadcast Management,* (Hastings House: New York, 1976), make the point that in order for a broadcaster to get support from his public on important issues, he must start by stimulating response on less important items. The broadcaster cannot expect sympathy, say Quaal and Brown, if he maintains a one-way system of communication. They contend that public apathy is a sign of poor management.

Public affairs programming is an ideal vehicle to promote two-way communication. You serve individuals and groups in the community by giving them a chance to air their ideas, promote civic projects, overcome community problems, solve crises and promote the general well-being of the community. Members of the community should have access to the station, have a chance to participate over the air, and have a chance to hear or see their interests covered by the station's programming.

These aims are accomplished in a variety of ways: audience participation programming, live coverage of events, editorials, political debates, documentaries, seminars for civic groups, religious news, appearances by station personalities or panel-interview programs.

It's Good Business

A number of broadcast executives interviewed during the preparation of this book point out the obvious advantages of being well known in any community. It's a whole lot easier to sell commercials, if the station is clearly recognized and well thought of by community members.

Joy Hoffer in his book, *Managing Today's Radio Station,* (TAB books No. 461) says: "Involvement in the community for the good of the community inevitably results in public cognizance of your efforts. Word gets around fast and your efforts will surely be rewarded in one way or another. Visualize the mileage that can come from it. Local media, trade publications, releases to your sales rep, and then maybe even an award for the station's accomplishments.

Your record of community involvement may be incorporated into any station sales presentation. Accordingly, your sales pitch takes on dimension and is not a mere repetition of ratings, rates and coverage. Community involvement produces an excitement factor that can only come from an inner feeling that you have benefited at least one other human being. By so benefiting him, you must benefit yourself."

It's important that a station which is doing good works tell everyone about them. There are many ways to gain recognition for outstanding public affairs efforts. This book includes a fairly extensive list of some of these possibilities.

Enlightened broadcasters recognize that it is in their best interest to do as much as well as they can in the public affairs field.

Chapter 2
Public Affairs Programming

Public affairs programming is becoming prominent in its own right. Long considered the bane of broadcasters' existence, it has now been found to be an audience builder and revenue producer. In addition, public affairs programming enhances a station's image.

Public affairs programs are becoming more imaginative. Formats are being developed which have broad appeal. These programs are being taken out of obscure time slots and moved to high-volume audience segments.

One key seems to be audience involvement. A number of formats have been developed which directly involve the public. Another key seems to be quality of production. A well-done documentary can command a significant audience, while a boring panel show will drive the audience away.

In this chapter we will describe some of the ways public affairs programming can be done with examples from a few specific programs. In the following two chapters we will look more closely at some public affairs programs which have received special recognition.

RADIO

When you study the public affairs programming on today's radio stations, you discover two major aspects. Number one is that radio is a two-way medium, in which the broadcaster and members of the audience share their ideas via the broadcast signal and the telephone. Number two is that people like to listen to other human voices. As a result some excellent documentary work is being done on radio by letting people relate their own experiences into the microphone and tape recorder.

Two-Way Talk

The two-way talk format on radio is so important that we will begin with a discussion of this technique and how it is being applied.

The idea of audience participation in a radio program has been around for a long time. In the earliest days of radio studio audiences were common, and there were scattered examples of man-on-the-street programs.

In the heyday of the disc jockey format, it was common to take music requests from the listening audience. Some stations began tape recording or even broadcasting live conversations with people who were requesting their favorite records. Pretty soon disc jockeys were taking calls from listeners and calling people in the listening audience, just to have zany conversations—or as part of station promotion contests.

Out of these early experiences came a new format—devised primarily to overcome the economic doldrums of late night and overnight hours, when many stations stayed on the air, but found little sponsor interest in the depleted, ill-defined; late-night audience.

The format was simple. Instead of playing records, a glib host, with a sense for current events and a flair for the dramatic, would go before the microphone and try to stir up responses from the audience. Listeners would call in and voice their opinions on any number of subjects. Occasionally, a studio guest would be interviewed by the host and engage in conversations with the callers.

The telephone-talk format prospered in metropolitan areas. Stations soon discovered that there was a large audience who enjoyed hearing other human voices discuss problems they had in common. More important from the view of station owners, revenues began to increase because station sales representatives could demonstrate that there was an audience for this type of format and they listened carefully and were involved in the broadcast. Soon sponsors began telling success stories based on their sponsorship of telephone-talk formats.

Out of these early experiments came some interesting developments. A good number of music-oriented stations turned over portions of their program time to talk shows, usually in the evening and overnight hours. One example was WBZ in Boston, a station noted for its music and news programming. WBZ hired a well-known talkmaster (talk show host) and soon prospered. Later a sports-oriented call-in show was added to the evening lineup.

A few stations tried talking all day. This format has had varying success, but there are prosperous stations using the all talk-radio format in major markets.

More recently the telephone-talk format has been adopted by stations in small markets to meet their own local needs. One popular application is to schedule a midday call-in show devoted to local and regional topics, mixing interviews with audience calls.

A specific example of a small market station using this technique to meet its own special needs is WSME in Sanford, Maine. Sanford is a southern Maine community of roughly 18,000 population. WSME is really two stations, a locally-oriented daylighter and a regionally-oriented FM.

WSME finds it can serve the Sanford-York County area best by scheduling a 30-minute, telephone-talk show from 12:30 p.m. to 1 p.m., Monday through Friday. Guests are invited to the studios three of the five days, but they must agree to accept calls from listeners. On the other two days the station holds what it calls an "open forum" during which listeners can discuss any issue on their mind.

WSME Vice-President and General Manager, Charlie Smith cited one of the attractions of the local program. "Every week we have one of the Sanford selectmen on one day to discuss town government."

General Manager Smith explained how a daytime only station solves its own special problems: "I think we start with a basic premise that public affairs programming does not have to be a tune-out and be buried at three in the morning, or broken up into one-and-a-half-minute segments, that you can sneak in and get enough time in to satisfy the FCC. We have found out that the 'speak out' program, which is what we call it, is definitely a plus factor for the station in terms of its position in the community." Of course, Smith also has to think about audience reaction to his public affairs programs—he can't bury a program intended for this daylight only AM station at 3 in the morning! So the program must be interesting.

Smith added: "Advertisers would request placement in or adjacent to 'speak out' and there's a definite feeling that even though we aren't like some of the big city stations, constantly lighting up boards full of phones, people in town really feel that 'speak out' is listened to...for example, we have a town meeting coming up...there's a lot of discussion of issues that are coming up on the program....and sit in the gallery (at the town meeting) and hear people getting up and saying 'Well, I heard on "speakout" that this...,' you get a real feel for what you can do in a community like this with this type of program."

WSME's Smith thinks the telephone talk format serves an important function in a small community, because it lets the people whose opinions are seldom heard express themselves, publicly. "There needs to be more man-on-the-street involvement," said Smith. "For every school board chairman and school superintendent, there are a lot of teachers and parents and so forth who have opinions about the schools; and it's very hard to get those brought out.

"We find that the telephone-talk format doesn't get 'em all calling," said Smith, "but we will get some of these other viewpoints from the non-establishment people, who are as important as anybody else."

One of the nation's outstanding community-oriented radio stations is WVOX in New Rochelle, New York. The Westchester County station has been honored many times for its vigorous pursuit of local affairs while operating in the shadow of 93 other metropolitan New York radio signals.

WVOX is a 500 watt daytimer with 3000 watts on FM. According to President Bill O'Shaughnessy, WVOX has less power than any other station in the New York market.

Part of the station's success is simply that of the 93 competitive signals, their format variations can be reduced to perhaps less than a dozen different approaches. O'Shaughnessy has made his station stand out from the braying herd.

WVOX programs directly to the many communities—residential, ethnic, cultural, religious, economic, etc.—within its coverage area.

The station makes considerable use of the telephone call-in format. According to O'Shaughnessy, the station's "bedrock, cornerstone" is "Westchester Open Line." He said: "Every day (Monday through Saturday) at ten o'clock in the morning we'll let anybody get on the air and have their say."

Sometimes there is a studio guest, frequently a government official, but the guest may be a personality drawn from a multitude of other fields, such as literature, theatre, consumer advocacy or education. On Wednesdays "Westchester Open Line" is concerned exclusively with New Rochelle, the city of license and one of the largest communities in the service area.

O'Shaughnessy advocates a sort of free form to radio programming. During a troubled time at New Rochelle High School, he ordered the "Open Line" extended to two hours (instead of one), and parents and teenagers were encouraged to call and discuss some of the issues which concerned them. WVOX routinely adjusts its programming on short notice to accommodate community needs.

The New Rochelle station has adapted the telephone-talk format to a number of other programs. A studio with telephone capability is available at all times, so little preparation is needed. For example, if desired, a Saturday noontime religious program could use an open line format for the discussion of religious topics, stimulated by a studio interview preceeding the call-in period.

Another suburban New York radio station which has built a national reputation for its public affairs programming is WRKL in Mt. Ida, Rockland County, New York.

Owner/manager Betty Ramey schedules an hour and a half, six days a week for telephone talk. Mrs. Ramey uses an unusual approach on some of her "Hot Line" programs, kicking off the program with an editorial which she voices, followed by an on-air response from someone representing an opposing viewpoint. Then the telephone lines are made available for comments from listeners.

"Hot Line" usually opens with a half-hour interview, followed by an hour for telephone calls. Mrs. Ramey estimates that on days when a guest appears, the station processes eight to 16 on-air telephone calls and on days when the program is thrown open to callers from the outset, as many as 16 to 24 calls are aired.

Mrs. Ramey described the typical content of a "Hot Line" program: "The supervisors of the town conduct business on the air, monthly. People can have them for an hour...on the air over issues that are irritating people. We've had hour-and-a-half programs, pro and con, for things like the abortion law amendments and ERA (the Equal Rights Amendment)."

During political seasons, the "Hot Line" program takes on an important function as a center for political debate.

Mrs. Ramey said: "Almost every office has an hour-and-a-half debate, among its candidates, on the air..." Some officials refuse to come, and WRKL clearly proclaims this fact to the audience. Other candidates refuse to face the barrage of telephone questioners and send in tape recordings setting forth their views. WRKL goes ahead and airs these tapes, but carefully announces that the candidate has declined to be interviewed and is providing a prepackaged statement.

The position of a local radio station as a forum for political debate is extremely important. In areas like the suburban New York counties we have just described, town, village and county candidates do not get exposure on the major metropolitan radio and television stations.

The only way their constituents have an opportunity to learn more about their positions on issues is through local media; and only the local radio station offers the opportunity for constituents to question a candidate directly without attending a rally or public forum.

The same problem pertains to rural areas where the metropolitan stations cannot cover local campaigns and newspaper coverage is thin. Local radio stations can, easily and inexpensively, open up local and regional political campaigns to the public through the use of the telephone call-in format.

A classic example of the telephone-talk format put to use in a major market is the experience of WDAE in Tampa, Florida. Tampa is a booming metropolitan market, ranked seventeenth in the nation by one survey organization.

WDAE was faced with the common problem of a radio station serving a strong television market. Both audience and sponsor interest had fallen off sharply in the evening during prime viewing hours.

The station hired an acknowledged expert in the telephone-talk format and scheduled a six-night-a-week talk show from eight to midnight. Former WDAE General Manager Donald K. Clark described the show: "(the host) does a shoot 'em up type show. (He) has guests on an average of two of his five week night shows. He likes to have what he calls an open forum...it's a no-holds barred conversation." The host often kicked off the show by talking about two or three of the day's leading news topics, sometimes voicing an opinion or two to stimulate phone calls.

WDAE used the telephone-talk format on Sunday nights for a different type of program. It was a non-controversial, public affairs block devoted to local programs and projects which needed support from the public. Usually, representatives of local public affairs organizations were interviewed and then the public would be encouraged to call in and discuss the particular project.

The telephone-talk format is versatile. It can be applied to a wide range of programs. While it is most often heard as a forum for political and social issues, such as taxation and abortion, there is no reason why a station can't use the telephone-talk format for a teenage program, religion, sports, educational topics, health matters, or any other specialized category which elicits sufficient interest to get telephone responses from listeners.

Some station managers are critical of telephone-talk formats, saying that, after a while, the same people seem to dominate the calls. In some cases, this may be an unavoidable truth and has caused some stations to drop the format. But it may be the fault of the topics and guests selected, and the skill of the program host.

Station managers might well look at some of the popular topics discussed on their telephone-talk program to see if they could be developed into other types of public affairs programs. For instance, if there's a great deal of interest every time a certain gardening expert appears, perhaps the station should develop a program dealing specifically with gardening, and sell it to compatible sponsors.

Documentaries

Radio documentaries fall into two categories—short and long. Many stations have developed a shortened version of the documentary program to meet special format needs.

One reason for brevity is a fear by station managers that any sustained documentary will drive the audience away, so they prefer to administer their documentaries in small doses.

Other stations schedule all their programs in brief segments and do mini-documentaries to fit into their format. This is an almost universal technique for all-news stations, which tend to limit all features to less than, say, four mintues.

For a long time, radio documentaries fell into disfavor...casualties of the disappearance of "programs" in favor of disc-jockey formats and the tightening of station budgets.

In recent years the news and public affairs aspect of radio has enjoyed a major rebirth and growth. The radio networks have continued to produce documentaries, and many individual stations are doing their own documentaries.

The CBS Radio Network provides affiliates with two types of documentaries. One is a once-a-month series which deals with one major topic such as taxation. This program runs about 24 minutes. The CBS Radio Network has also built a considerable reputation in the documentary field with saturation of mini-documentaries on weekends. The network's regular features are replaced by documentary features. A theme is selected for the whole series of programs, and then a specific topic is assigned to each segment. For example, a series on developments in medicine might be broken into programs on major disease areas such as kidney and heart disease, as well as on specific developments in medical treatment or service.

The same techniques are used by local stations. Station WRFM in New York City has a regular series of time slots set aside for its mini-documentaries. The segments are aired three times a day, five days a week. The series has a generic title, but specific topics within the series may have sub-titles such as "Crime in the streets."

All-news WCBS in New York is less structured. During a major project dealing with law and the courts, the station aired segments of its mini-documentaries daily, and then combined the segments into longer programs for repeat use on the weekend. In addition the station aired an hour-long open forum—Friday morning of each week during the series—to permit experts and members of the public to discuss the topics which had been brought up during the week. The mini-documentary series, the forum and the summary reports were all repeated during the 24-hour broadcast day to assure maximum exposure.

Producing a Documentary. The word documentary tends to strike fear in the hearts of station managers and news directors. To the station manager the word documentary brings on visions of vast sums of money pouring from an unregulated financial faucet. To news directors, the visions are of 28-hour days extending off into infinity. Neither fear must be realized.

A radio documentary can be produced quite economically. After all, the basic element of most documentaries is the interview. Most stations already have portable tape recorders, the most popular being the battery-operated cassette machines. Audiotape is certainly a minimal expense item. A documentary can be produced with rudimentary production facilities, although having the capability to mix tape by using a console and three tape recorders has distinct advantages.

The most important rule for a news or public affairs director, given the assignment of developing a documentary is first think about the topic. Do some reading and telephoning to research the topic. Find out if you can get some concerned organizations to do some leg work for you.

If, for example, you are doing a mini-documentary series on health facilities in your community:

Sit down and list all the facilities you can think of. Then leaf through the telephone book, municipal and state directories, and any other directories you have around to see if you've forgotten any facilities. (The American Society of Association Executives and the Public Relations Society of America both publish excellent directories, which are available in some libraries.) Make a list of the organizations involved in health care. For example: your county and state medical societies, the American Medical Association, the American Hospital Association. You would list governmental organizations such as the municipal, county and state health departments, medical colleges in your area, health-study groups, such as the health facilities committee of your local League of Women Voters or good government organization. Perhaps the local anti-poverty groups have a special interest in health matters. Certainly any senior citizens groups will be interested. There may even be a health facilities' coordinating agency in your area.

Once you have compiled a long list of places, people and organizations which have something to do with health, go back and study your topic outline. Do you know what specific questions you want to look into? Is your topic too broad, or too narrow?

Perhaps you will decide that what you really want to know is how the health facilities within your coverage area are being utilized. Are they efficient or are there duplications? Are rates exorbitant for services rendered? Are facilities lacking, or improperly utilized? Are emergency services and clinics adequate? How is the tax dollar being spent? Are facilities for the elderly and indigent adequate and convenient?

Check your list for people and organizations which relate to your narrowed topic.

If you have given yourself enough lead time before the anticipated air date of the program, write a personal form letter and mail it to the organizations which you think can provide you with helpful literature and contacts. Typically, these would include the major associations, state offices, federal offices and educational institutions. Many of these letters will result in your receiving piles of literature, background booklets, sets of professional standards and other information, which you can use to measure local performance of health facilities.

Local organizations should be contacted by telephone. You will undoubtedly be given specific suggestions on individuals you should talk with; and you will uncover some of the issues which concern people in your local health establishment. You should also uncover some issues which have sharply-divided opinions, and you will probably gather more literature for both sides, including copies of surveys and studies.

At this point, sit down and digest all that you have learned up to now. Go over your preliminary outline and start matching up the information you have gathered with your original set of objectives. Have you left anything out? Is there an element you at first thought was important that now seems less so? Whom should you interview?

Make up your list of potential interviews and begin lining up appointments. (It is best, if at all possible, to do in-person, as opposed to telephone, interviews, both for tape quality and because they are usually more productive.)

The personal interview also permits you to make acquaintances who may be valuable for later public affairs and news coverage. (It may also be possible for you to discharge some of the station's ascertainment requirements under the FCC rules, a point which we will elaborate on in Chapter 5.)

There will be spin-offs from these interviews. You will end up interviewing individuals not on your original list but these interviews may be the best ones you do. Don't limit your interviewing to just the "experts" or to the leaders. Talk to anyone who has some interest in the matters you are covering in your documentary. After all, your documentary is aimed at the general public. They will identify more quickly with their peers than the select few who run the organizations or hold political office.

As you do your interviewing, think about ambient sound. Ambient sound is the background sound that's just there when you do an interview. Let your tape recorder run before and after the interview, without anyone speaking, so that you have some ambient sound available to edit in, later on. It sounds better when you insert some tape of ambient sound into a narration, if you fade up the background under the narration first and then fade it down. You may even end up using the background sound throughout the whole feature, if it isn't too long.

Be sure to look specifically for opportunities to record pure background for activity sound. If you are in a hospital, record the sounds of the waiting rooms, the corridors, the nursing stations, any equipment you hear and perhaps even the food preparation area.

Perhaps the biggest problem in producing a radio documentary is curbing your desire to do more and more. Set practical limits for yourself, based on time, staff and facilities, and do your best to stay somewhere inside these limits.

One of the most time-consuming aspects is the digesting of the interviews you have done. If it is possible, get the key parts of the interviews transcribed. This permits you to write a script and cut tape according to the transcript. If you don't transcribe, make good notes, with suggested in-cues and out-cues and details as to what was said.

Then outline the specific program you want to do. This outline is for script purposes. You must think out what you want to cover, what interviews and sound effects you want to use, and what background material you will need.

Then comes the hard work, sitting down and writing a script. There is no set way to script a program, but modern radio theory puts great emphasis on including the voices of the people who are important to the discussion of your topic. Thus, most scripts become a sort of road map, leading us from tape insert to tape insert with some elaboration as we go along. It is a challenging and difficult assignment because it calls for skillful integration of the text and tape—or the final product will sound "choppy."

We won't give a course in broadcast writing here, but remember, what you write is to be read aloud/and listened to, rather than to be read silently. Sentence fragments and odd phraseology are permissible, if they "sound" OK.

Don't give up until you have made your point clear, understandable and, if possible, dramatic.

You may even find that the bulk of your documentary or documentaries can be made up of skillfully edited cuts of tape, in which the people involved tell the story themselves.

Of everything needed to produce a radio documentary the most important commodity is time. If you can't devote large chunks of time to your program close to the air date, then plan to do your work a little bit at a time way in advance. Time can be apportioned effectively, if you think out every step of your project.

Another rule: simplicity is not evil. It's better to do a simple, balanced exposition of some important local issue than to ignore that issue. It's better to run a series of well-done and well-edited interviews with an appropriate introduction and close, than to ignore an issue.

For example, your community is embroiled in a fight over a bond issue for improvement of the water system. At the very least, interview all the relevant spokepersons and write a script explaining the issue and who each person is. Put each spokesperson on in a separate mini-program and re-explain the issue each time, so that if someone listens to your station over several hours or several days, they can get a representative sampling of the major viewpoints on the bond issue. This is not a pure documentary, but it beats forgetting about the whole thing.

Of course, there are other ways to accomplish this same objective. You could invite all the disputants in for a telephone-talk panel show. You could interview each person on the news. One way to be certain that the issue is discussed in isolation from other topics is to put together a series of brief programs on the bond issue and let everyone have his say. Then follow it up with a program involving public participation after major viewpoints have been expressed, so that the listening audience can discuss specific questions.

Documentaries—long or short—have a special meaning to radio stations. They tend to stand alone, bringing audience recognition and prestige to the station. And, if the station does an aggressive and skillful job of promoting itself, it can reap awards which will enhance its standing in the community and in the profession. All of this is pertinent in the eyes of the FCC and the local community, within professional organizations, and in the recruitment of high caliber employees. We will talk at greater length about promotion and winning recognition in Chapter 10.

Public Affairs Features

Public affairs features are usually short programs which the listener or viewer can expect to hear or see at a specific time. They serve to educate or inform and, usually, deal with only one topic.

Some examples:

- a program on health topics
- a program on minority issues
- school lunch menus
- a listing of entertainment events
- a feature on education

There is no end to the possibilities for developing public affairs features. Any interesting topic of fairly broad public interest is adaptable to this sort of feature, and in many cases is highly saleable to sponsors.

The production of public affairs features can be designed to fit the financial and staff requirements of the particular station.

A metropolitan station might produce a program on health topics by using a producer and a technician to conduct and edit interviews, and prepare scripts. A station in a smaller market might rely on an accepted local medical authority who would prepare his or her own script and material.

Sometimes all that is needed is a routine call to the station. For instance, if a station wished to list the school lunch menus for the week, all that would be needed is an agreement with the school system to have someone send in the list or call the station in advance of the air date. Since this sort of information is planned well in advance, this presents no problem.

In thinking about public affairs features, first consider some of the topics of broad general interest such as: health, education, child care and raising, business, taxation and finance, problems of the elderly, problems of the handicapped, sports and recreation. The list could go on for pages.

There are specific needs within each community, though, and a station's management should be able to define these areas of special interest. A sunbelt community with a high proportion of retired residents might want to develop features having to do with recreation, transportation, health matters and financial assistance available to the senior citizen. A community in which a significant number of residents are non-English speaking might have a need for a news program in, say, Spanish, French or some other language.

Fortunately, there is a wealth of outside help available in preparing and airing public affairs features. In New York City, the media situation is so complex that private foundation money is funding an organization to promote public understanding of school topics by acting as an intermediary between the school system and the metropolitan area's radio and television stations. The group defines problems and assists stations in producing features on the schools.

Most communities have plenty of people and organizations available to help. The parent/teachers association might be willing to assist in lining up topics on education. Perhaps a local college or university has faculty resources. Most fund-raising groups, such as the Red Cross and United Fund, have staff members who can assist stations. And today, many municipal, county and state governments have experts trained to help the media. As an example —most state agriculture departments and state university extension services are well equipped to assist in preparing public affairs features, both for farmers and gardeners.

Most public affairs features are simple in format. Often they consist of a brief script prepared and delivered by an expert or by a station staff member. Sometimes the script is simply a wrap-around—an introduction and a conclusion to a topical interview.

Public service features not only discharge an obligation under a station's license commitment, but they are important image builders.

Service to the community is thought by many progressive broadcasters to be a keynote to a station's success. No matter what the format of a station, there is a place for public affairs features. Of course they must be tailored to the station's audience and to the station's format.

If a station operates with a tightly-produced music format aimed at teens and young 20s, then it should select topics of interest to these groups and produce brief, tight features to insert between segments of music.

An all-news station is apt to cover a broader spectrum and do a more sophisticated, more journalistic type of public service or public affairs feature. This sort of station usually has the staff, expertise and broad range of audience to warrant this approach.

Stations managers should regularly evaluate their public affairs features, to see if some need replacing and others need updating to meet new needs. From time to time, stations develop new features to meet needs they discover through their ascertainment programs (see Chapter 5).

Live Broadcasts

Trends in broadcasting, like everything else, have a tendency to run in cycles. During the heyday of pre-television radio, live broadcasts were considered routine, even live remote broadcasts.

Then, for a long time, live broadcasts were infrequent, except for coverage of sports events and personal appearances by disc jockeys at store openings, etc.

We've already pointed out that one form of live studio broadcasting is very popular today, the telephone-talk program. But the live remote is returning to the airwaves. One reason is the improved economic strength of radio and the originality of station programmers.

Also, live broadcasts can now be done inexpensively. One objection frequently raised by managers is the cost of renting an adequate telephone remote line from the location of the remote to the studio. Depending on local union situations, stations managers also question the labor costs involved.

Today, there are a number of transmission alternatives available. One is the use of two-way radio. Many radio stations now are equipped with high-quality, two-way radio equipment. Often it is used, primarily, by the news department to allow reporters to communicate quickly and easily with the newsroom. But the two-way radio has many other uses. Depending on the equipment ordered, it is possible to do lengthy remotes by radio alone.

In fact, this facility is so valuable that any station owner or manager considering the purchase of two-way equipment should investigate the added cost involved in installing equipment which can be used for sustained broadcasts. The cost may be written off by the elimination of expensive telephone company lines.

In considering the purchase of two-way equipment, take a close look at the area you need to cover and the nature of the terrain. If your remote sportscasts all take place many miles from the station, or your most likely areas for broadcasting a speech are not in good line-of-sight locations, then the equipment may not help you enough to warrant buying it.

Two-way radio equipment not only saves telephone line rentals, it permits rapid set-ups when you reach the broadcast location. It also avoids the hazards of finding that the telephone company has either failed to install a line, or has put the terminal in the wrong place.

The equipment can be made extremely flexible. Some stations use a transceiver from the remote location to the mobile unit; and use the mobile unit to rebroadcast the signal to the station.

There are other ways to do a remote broadcast. One rather hazardous technique is to take along a good quality battery-operated tape recorder, a good pencil mike with a windshield, a set of alligator clips and set up the equipment by attaching the clips to a nearby telephone—which you've taken apart for the occasion. (This is done by unscrewing the mouthpiece of the telephone and attaching the two alligator clips to the two little prongs inside the mouthpiece. The other end of the clip apparatus plugs into a tape recorder output.)

We said this method was hazardous, if expedient. One hazard is that the telephone company will have put epoxy on the mouthpiece, making it virtually impossible to twist off (unless you have the appropriate type of wrench.)

There's always the possibility that someone will break the connection or the batteries might die. This technique will help you in news emergencies. Network reporters who file features from various locations often use this method of feeding. They record their feature on a cassette, and then hook the recorder up to the telephone and play the cassette to a production studio where it is rerecorded and edited.

One network covered the Olympics using similar equipment; and just telephoned in its Olympic reports to the master control room. Some quality was lost, but there was a considerable saving over the cost of renting lines from the remote location.

One device—a VoiceAct—which is very handy and quite adaptable also uses the telephone. Again, you unscrew the mouthpiece cover, and attach the device directly on in place of the mouthpiece cover. The device acts as a miniature microphone and amplifier, and can be used to do a remote simply by plugging in the remote equipment.

Some stations simply install a business telephone and do remotes. This is also a good idea for news coverage from locations where the station may want to establish fast communications, such as at city hall. The telephone company installs a wall outlet where the station wants it, and the phone is kept locked up until it is needed. Then, it is simply plugged into the wall outlet.

So, there are a variety of ways to do a live broadcast. The next question is—what do you broadcast live?

There are plenty of opportunities—and one major pitfall: A live broadcast needs to have enough noise and excitement to be interesting—to sound "live."

A number of station managers say they have given up live broadcasts of local legislative sessions, such as the city council or county commissioners. In general, these sessions tend to be long, involved and incorporate language and terms which mean little or nothing to the average listener. It is far better to send a member of the news staff to sit and listen, and then interpret what happens for the audience. Some stations tape sessions of the city council or board of aldermen for excerpting by the news department, but most stations are cautious about live coverage of public meetings.

Charlie Smith of WSME in Sanford, Maine explained why his station doesn't broadcast the representative town meeting. He says by the time of the meeting it's too late. He says you have to bring the material out in advance in order to get people stirred up enough to consult with their town meeting members—and give them any chance to influence what's going to happen in the town meeting.

Smith invites town officials to appear on his station's telephone-talk program to take calls from constituents prior to the representative town meeting.

Live broadcasts, however, are particularly adaptable to special events. For instance, if a town is celebrating its centennial, there will be a number of festivities during the upcoming weekend and plenty of opportunities to broadcast live. You could broadcast the opening ceremonies...the parade... the reenactment of a historic event....

There are some speeches which warrant local coverage. Most stations would broadcast a speech by the President, even if it were largely of a laudatory nature. And, during major political campaigns, many stations broadcast major speeches in their localities by significant candidates. In addition, stations aggressively seek to gather the candidates together for debates—either under the auspices of a civic group or in their own studios.

Donald Clark, former general manager of WDAE in Tampa, Florida recalls the station's experience with live political debates. He said: "We started...on a small scale (We asked the University of Tampa to give us their auditorium)...we invited a group of city council candidates and found that we invited too many... we had to learn that you cannot get into this area of letting everybody say something, so we changed our philosophy and said from now on, we will pick out one or two races...and let them ask each other questions."

Clark added: "We got one of these that turned out pretty well and we moved into the bank building downtown, where they have a large cafeteria. (They were interested in promoting the idea.) We filled that place and we allowed some of the people who came, to ask questions right there on the spot....they could ask the candidate questions...it proved to be pretty popular with the people, but not with the candidates....I think it's proven to be a real winner for the station."

There are, of course, many ways to set up a debate format. Clark points out one noteworthy fact: A local college or university can be invaluable in developing this sort of program, even down to the availability of needed broadcast and public address equipment.

WCBS in New York City has won national recognition for a series of child-care seminars it conducted, called "A Right to Life." The seminars themselves were all-day affairs at a college or medical center. Periodically, during the day, a WCBS reporter would do live cut-ins from the seminar to highlight some of the major topics discussed.

WCBS has taken some of its forums out into the community, arranging for a panel to meet at a public auditorium to answer questions from the audience during a live broadcast.

Another group which is extremely helpful in setting up programs having to do with government or politics is the League of Women Voters. This volunteer organization has developed considerable expertise on local, state and national issues, and can be invaluable to a station wishing to set up a public forum on a political-governmental topic.

Station management should be alert to those sudden and unexpected opportunities to go live, when such a broadcast will serve a public need and demonstrate the station's high degree of community involvement.

A classic example would be an emergency situation—a tornado has struck, poisonous gas is leaking from a railroad tank car, a forest fire threatens the community. These are situations in which radio excells. There are situations when a radio station should be capable of going live from remote locations.

There are also on-the-spot news coverage, live news conferences, announcements by public officials, instructions from emergency organizations. There can be no excuse for laying back and playing records when these types of situations occur.

Another example: There is trouble on the streets; teenagers acting out against the community. There's news coverage, but then, what can a station do next? Perhaps a rap session or forum involving teens, adults, educators and community officials. The station's telephone-talk capabilities should be exploited to stimulate discussion of the situation. And the station would immediately begin investigating the root causes of the community's problem, with the idea of producing something of a documentary nature.

Remember that radio is a very personal medium. It relies on human voices communicating to individual human ears, and radio is seldom better than when it is live and spontaneous.

The Interview Show

Perhaps the oldest public affairs format is the interview show. Across the land there are hundreds of copies of "Face the Nation" or "Meet the Press."

The interview show is a simple program to product. It requires only enough microphones to go around for the panel and the guest or guests.

The secret to producing a top-notch interview program is to have a sharp panel, a guest who talks well, and topics which are interesting or controversial.

It's always easier to interview someone who has something to say about topics which are foremost in the public's mind. This is easier to accomplish in larger communities than in small ones, where the number of issues facing public discussion may be few and far between.

One solution to making the program interesting is to expand your spectrum. Instead of relying solely on interviews with political leaders, consider the potential of interviewing the president of the local college, the director of the state's environmental program, or the president of a major local industry. Interviews don't have to be restricted to political and governmental issues. They can be done on religion, health, education and other topics.

The major fault of most panel shows is that they lack preparation. The moderator and the panel should know something about the interviewee—the person's background, where he or she stands on some current issues, his or her involvement in a local controversy, etc.

The next major fault of panel shows is timidity. The guest is there to be questioned vigorously. He or she is not likely to be naive. You invited the guest there to be asked difficult questions, and you can assume the guest is willing to face them. Encourage your panels to do their homework and come up with hard-hitting questions, which are based on issues that you know concern your audience.

Another major fault of most interview shows is the failure of the panel to follow up on good questions. Too often, another panel member is so anxious to voice his or her question that the guest avoids having to answer a detailed follow-up question.

Another oversight by many stations is their failure to realize that a good panel show generates news. A member of the news department should listen to the program for possible excerpts to be included in the news. If the news department has an opportunity to preview a taped panel show, you can effectively promote the program simply by including small portions of the guest's comments in the newscasts. You should also consider having excerpts from the program available for use on following newscasts. If your program is scheduled for Sunday night, you might be able to use short excerpts from the program on the Monday morning news. You may very well have one of the strongest stories in your region or state, so put it to good use.

Some stations even send transcripts or excerpts of their programs to the state bureaus of the wire services, realizing that, from time to time, the wires will pick up on something in these programs and write a story which mentions the station's call letters. This sort of publicity is good for the station's image and helps in getting other important guests to agree to appear.

Select your panel members carefully. Usually, its a good idea to have the moderator and at least one other member of the panel from the station's staff. Then, if need be, you can rely on a reputable outside person as the third questioner; (three seems to be an optimum number of questioners for radio).

Quiz Shows

Quiz shows aren't totally dead on radio. While they may not work too well as entertainment features, they can become viable as public affairs formats. An educational radio network in the south programs a quiz in which two groups of students, representing different high schools, compete for the honor and glory of winning.

The same sort of thing could be done with adults, using topical questions.

Mixed Techniques

It has probably become obvious that various public affairs formats can be intermixed to increase the impact of your programming. One of the more obvious combinations is the public affairs interview used as a lead-off for a telephone call-in format.

And we've mentioned the use by some stations of a public forum or a call-in show and panel to supplement a mini-documentary series.

As you can see, the various formats can be mixed to increase the effectiveness of your public affairs effort and to get more use out of the time and effort you invest in this area.

Weather

Radio stations broadcast weather reports throughout the day. However, there's a tendency to overlook two aspects of weather reporting. The first is features on weather. Meteorologist Gordan Branes has done features on weather patterns and weather lore on the CBS Radio Network for a number of years. There's no reason why a local station with a staff or contract meteorologist couldn't develop a regular weather feature, with special attention to important local conditions, such as the effects of weather on gardens, farms and recreational areas.

The second, often neglected, aspect of weather reporting is preparedness for weather emergencies. Every station should be prepared to swing into action in the face of severe weather—tornadoes, hurricanes, snow storms. There should be a notification system, a plan for staffing, provisions for obtaining weather reports and condition reports, perhaps (if it's available in your area) a monitor to receive the National Weather Service's radio broadcast. In any area where weather makes news consistently, a station should consider spending the additional money to obtain a regular weather wire to supplement it's news wire service.

TELEVISION

The major difference between the public affairs programming of a radio station and that of a television station is in the area of documentaries. Television is an extraordinary medium because it allows the consumer to see, rather than imagine what people and localities look like. The documentary is really the skillful use of sight and sound to tell a story. Documentaries are done on radio, but they do require a degree of imagination from the listener which is eliminated by the television picture.

Studio Programs

Studio programs, for the sake of this discussion, are programs done live or on tape in facilities within the confines of the station building. The emphasis is usually on the "live" quality of the program, even if it is recorded on tape.

The most-copied format would have to be the news panel interview, patterned on those network standbys: "Face the Nation," "Meet the Press" and "Issues and Answers."

The panel interview show is a mainstay of television public affairs. It is a good solid format which deserves care and concern from the station's management. It also deserves slotting in favorable program times—which doesn't mean Sunday morning at nine o'clock.

The usual format is to invite one, or perhaps two, guests and have them interviewed by a panel of journalists, including journalists from outside the interviewing organization.

Some of the topics which might be discussed include: mass transit, taxation, the plight of the schools, race relations, court-ordered busing for integration, corruption in government, crime on the streets, public housing policy, cancer detection and research, abortion, women's rights, minority employment, consumer fraud, gambling and on and on and on.

Here is where the station's program to uncover community issues and needs comes into play. The FCC calls this procedure ascertainment—finding out what community leaders and the public in general, think are community issues. The station should attempt to coordinate the topics of public concern uncovered in ascertainment surveys with guests for public affairs programs.

There are three elements to a good panel show. The first is getting a good guest. This means someone who is the object of current interest, who will speak coherently and interestingly, and who has something important to say. This is the time to invite the people who make the news—meaning the people who make decisions and who make policy.

They could include the senators and representatives in Congress, the key state legislators, mayors, city council members, city and county managers, county judges and commissioners, state and federal officials, top business leaders, legal, medical, educational and religious leaders.

In addition you might ask leaders of minority groups, scientists, ex-convicts, practically anyone who can speak out on important community issues. The list is far longer than you might expect.

The second element to a good panel show is having a good panel. It used to be that the panel always included one or two newspaper journalists because of their supposed greater depth of knowledge about certain topics. This is far less a necessity today, as broadcast reporters have become better educated, trained amd more specialized in their reporting assignments.

Today, many television stations can field a political specialist, a consumer reporter and a science and medicine specialist.

The panel's moderator is usually one of the station's anchor reporters. From the management's point of view it makes good sense to utilize a highly paid, anchor reporter for this additional task; and most anchorpeople welcome the opportunity to do a panel show for the change of pace and the intellectual challenge.

You should find the balance of reporters which best fits your time, facilities and format. Often a moderator and two or three additional reporters is a good combination. You will find that certain people work well together and after a while, you will be able to select panelists who complement each other. It's often good to seek a degree of contrast. An easy-going, almost solicitous reporter can be balanced with a real get-to-the-heart-of-it bulldog type.

One panel on which the author served became quite effective by balancing the anchorman-moderator who was an excellent political reporter and generalist, with a newspaper reporter who knew the inner workings of politics and two other station reporters—one of whom would ask general questions framed from the perspective of an average viewer. The other reporter would bore in with the "no baloney" type of question. Most guests ended up praising the panel for its thoroughness and insight while admitting they had really been put through the wringer.

The third element is follow-through. The moderator plays an essential role here. Too often, on this type of program, when a good question is asked, the guest gives a partial or too-general answer, and the follow-up question is dropped. Sometimes it is because no one thinks to ask the follow-up or because someone is eager to move on to another line of questioning. The moderator needs to be alert to make sure that important questions and answers are followed up. The reporters also bear the responsibility to keep the guest from sloughing off the initial question with an incomplete answer. After all, the point to this sort of program is to dig a little deeper into topics of current concern.

While guests should be treated courteously, there is no reason not to ask hard, factual, well-documented questions which need to be answered properly to inform the public. The people who agree to appear on these programs know the risks, and while they probably assume they can confuse and becloud matters on which they prefer not to elaborate, they also know that, if pressed, they will have to answer the questions. After all, even if the guest doesn't give a complete answer, if it seems obvious that there is an element of evasion, then you've brought out something which the public should think about, when it comes time to vote or write letters.

One difficulty of producing a news panel show is that it's best to not book all your interviews far in advance of the recording and air times. While it's reassuring to you and your staff to know you have the show "in the can" and ready to go, you need the flexibility to cover topics of current concern when they crop up.

If for example, the transit authority comes out with a study which recommends building a massive subway system to serve your metropolitan area, you shouldn't wait a month to interview someone on this topic. You should be on the air during the next week with a good solid news panel show, interviewing the top transit official on the specifics of the plan. On other programs, and in future weeks on your regularly scheduled news panel show, you should interview officials and experts who hold contrasting views.

The next step is difficult for many stations, but you should arrange some way to get at least a portion of the transcript of the show into the hands of both wires services—AP and UPI—for possible inclusion in their weekend coverage.

Since well-done interview programs of the type we're discussing often generate news, it's important to make sure that their contents get to the wire services. The services will be eager to pick up on newsmaking responses to your questions to enhance the prior week's stories or set up a story for the coming week if the topic is of current concern. And the services scrupulously credit the source of the material which means your station will get print and broadcast plugs in state and regional wire service reports, as well as the media. This doesn't hurt your image one bit.

The best way to handle the wire service contact is to make a written transcript of the entire program. This is time consuming and expensive and, thus, is done in only a few cases. This type of program is often recorded near the close of business on Friday, or for that matter, may be broadcast live on Saturday or Sunday. It is then difficult to get an immediate transcript typed up in time for concurrent use on the wire services.

The next best thing to do is to view the show, and decide on two or three important excerpts. These can then be transcribed and either sent or phoned to the wire services, often by the newsroom personnel.

To get more media coverage, stations which have joint radio and television facilities should consider the possibility of broadcasting the same program on both facilities, even, perhaps, by sharing personnel. Many stations excerpt small portions of these interviews for insertion in their news, especially on these eternally-difficult to fill Saturday and Sunday evening newscasts and on Monday morning newscasts, if such exist. Sometimes, the excerpt is balanced by a similar-length comment from an opponent of the idea expressed, or the person criticized in the original interview.

It might even be possible for the radio news staff to provide audio cuts for use by other stations either by feeding a regional network, the regional wire service audio network (if there is one), or by feeding the excerpts to any station wishing to call yours collect. (Put out a note over the wires that you are willing to do this—providing they credit your station, of course.)

This kind of promotion of your programs can enhance your station's image. In every state there are some stations which consistently draw attention to themselves for the excellence and topicality of their new interview panels. And they are not always the largest or metropolitan stations. They are the stations that plan, get good guests, put together intelligent panels and ask probing questions. Then these stations make the maximum use of their material for on-air news and for promotion of their own image by distribution of program excerpts.

Just think how the major morning paper in your city would look with a lead story quoting a political leader interviewed on your program. Opinion makers and advertisers would preceive this irony, we're sure.

Other Interviews

Another staple of television public affairs programming is the news or community interest interview within the confines of a regularly scheduled program. The granddaddy of them all is the "Today" show. This idea has since been copied by stations all over the country, in many cases with great success.

Typically these programs are slotted in the early or mid-morning hours, although there is a new movement to so-called "magazine" shows in the early evening, before network prime time begins.

With this sort of format you can select topics from a broad spectrum. The program can discuss how to right the red ant infestation on one day and ask the district attorney why he hasn't pursued the prosecution of a certain important official on the next day. There are hundreds of topics of interest to your viewers. All you need is to have someone designated to dream them up and find the people to talk about them.

The two major weaknesses in most programs of this sort is that they tend to cover a multiple of subjects; and thus, some of the interviews are too short to explore the topic fully. In some cases this is intentional. Some station managers or owners fear having their hosts roll up their sleeves (figuratively) and really discuss important issues.

Why pussy-foot around about the abortion issue? Sure, someone out there is going to be upset—no matter what your guest says. But that's part of your job—to stimulate public discussion of issues which are important to members of your community—even if you have to stand a little gaff from your critics.

The FCC has made it exceedingly clear that this is what the long-term objective of the Fairness Doctrine is—a full and adequate discussion of all topics of community concern. You don't have to editorialize if you don't wish to, but no broadcaster has the right to shut off the discussion of vital community issues.

What kills the effectiveness of any interview is a poor interviewer. All too frequently hosts on the sort of mixed entertainment and information program we've been talking about, simply don't have the background or the time to prepare a meaningful interview.

The worst thing that can happen is to hand the microphone over to the guest and let him talk. This is the communications business, which means that the broadcaster should be guiding the questioning so the audience gets something useful out of the interview.

The author's pet peeve is the "back-patter" interview. There is no sane reason to waste your valuable broadcast time patting someone on the back. If you think it will promote sales—it's time to ask yourself whether or not your sales department is effective.

The joy of having available programs on which you can schedule interviews is that it presents a wide variety of possibilities to you. Think, for instance, what you could do if some really distinguished person dropped in—an astronaut, the vice-president of the United States, a famous opera star. If you have a regularly scheduled program, you could program an extended live or taped interview. The audience building and image enhancing aspects alone boggle one's mind.

It's a good idea to tape any live interview, off the air, if you think it will have any potential for inclusion in the day's newscasts. For example, if you do a current news interview on your morning show, why not include a clip from it in the noontime news? And if you have developed a magazine format (a program made up of several self-contained packages, such as CBS' "60 Minutes"), you might develop something worth using on the late evening news.

The keys to doing good interviews are selecting topics of interest to your viewers; selecting (at least occasionally) topics which stimulate discussion or controversy; and selecting a well-informed, skilled interviewer.

You might also consider the possibility of an occasional guest interviewer. For example, your station does its own morning program with a regular interview guest appearing each day. If your interviewee happens to be involved in a hot local political issue, why not have someone from the news department do the interview, rather than the host. You will probably improve the quality of the interview, and provide your news department with a morale-building stimulus which will go a long way to build spirit among your newspeople. If the topic is farming, invite the farm director. The "CBS Morning News" uses this technique—using the anchorpersons and a specialized reporter to interview the guest, in a modified form of the panel interview.

There are many, many other ways to use the interview format. It can beef up what is often a sagging noontime news program. You can build programs around specific areas of community interest, such as sports, religion, agriculture, youth services to the elderly, or education. And in most cases there are non-profit organizations serving these constituencies, which would be most willing to lend whatever assistance needed in defining issues, locating guests, providing interview panel members or running extension meetings in the community, based on your broadcasts. Often these groups will pick up expenses such as printing literature needed to inform listeners or the cost of mailing publicity releases.

The Quiz Program

We think of quiz programs in terms of the daily daytime quiz shows or the once-a-week early evening syndicated programs. But the quiz format is an old standby in the public affairs area.

One of the most common applications is to invite two groups of high school students into the studios and have them answer general knowledge questions. This type of program is designed to stimulate respect for academic achievement. In a way, it serves as somewhat of a measure of the accomplishment of various school systems since members of the audience can't help but wonder why certain schools fare better than others, or why today's youngsters can't spell. If properly thought out and produced, this sort of program can stimulate local audience interest, and it serves to bring the station into contact with various communities at a very personal level. Especially in small and medium-sized markets, there's nothing like having as many people as possible tour your production facilities...or have a member of their family on your program...to establish a rapport with your audience.

The quiz format is most often tied to an educational institution because you can get expert advice with the questions. Usually the teams represent schools because it's easier to organize the competition, and you have some assurance that the participants will be familiar with the general subject matter. The same idea can be applied to other organized groups, such as the 4-H Clubs.

Religion

It's almost trite to mention that an overwhelming proportion of television stations schedule one or two brief sermonettes daily, usually at sign-on and sign-off. These are usually rotated throughout the clerical community in the viewing area so that everyone gets an opportunity to be represented.

A few stations have televised religious services from their own studios; and others go out to houses of worship with their remote units.

There's always the religious discussion program and the semi-magazine format in which you may feature a choir or musical group, an interview and a direct talk by the cleric, all on the same program.

And in a few instances, there are some very stimulating programs aimed at certain target audiences, such as children.

Agriculture

In areas where agriculture plays an important part in the economy, television stations usually schedule specific programs of interest to farmers and agri-business people. Some simply air programs prepared by outside organizations, such as the state agricultural extension service.

Others air their own programs, which are frequently flexible enough to allow for studio interviews, demonstrations, or film or tape inserts.

It's common practice on stations which have a farm director to have this individual host the program. To a great extent the quality of these programs is governed by the amount of time and effort the station is willing to put into them. If there are sufficient personnel available to line up interviews and demonstrations, and to go out and do special filming or taping, these programs can be very interesting and informative.

Fortunately, there are plenty of organizations around who can help out—one, of course, being the agricultural extension service. Others are the agriculture college at the state university, the state experimental stations, various universities which do agricultural research, the 4-H Club, the Grange, the Farm Bureau and agri-business firms.

Unfortunately, some stations don't provide for adequate production time, so the farm show ends up with the farm director doing a dull interview with the head of the local Agricultural Stabilization and Conservation Service office.

There's a lot of politics to farming and it would seem that there could be a great deal more discussion of controversial topics. If you want to stir up a little discussion in the community, just invite Oren Lee Staley of the National Farmers Organization or some other equally militant farm leader in. All too frequently stations tiptoe away from discussion of views held by radical farm groups, as well as those held by the ultra-conservative wing or by consumer groups. How about talking about price supports and the "big business" of juggling federal programs to make a profit? Then there's the whole issue of sales to foreign nations—or the role of the commodity markets. There are plenty of topics which farmers want to know more about.

How about changes in the merchandising of agricultural products, or innovations in shipping or changes in the marketing pattern? Is your farm department keeping its constituency informed on trends which may have long-term effects on farm and agri-business people in your area?

Then, there's the matter or agricultural education. What's being done to train the next generation for careers in agriculture? What are the trends, what skills will be required, is farming going to be a viable way of life for today's youngsters ?

How about the economics and technology of farming? Do you ever send the farm director off to farm equipment conventions? Do you conduct seminars for area farmers on tax legislation, or innovations in the handling of the crops common to your area? How about farm safety training? Or, do you help farmers learn more about complying with government regulations which affect them?

There are almost unlimited possibilities for good solid farm-oriented programming. And there's no reason why it has to go unsponsored. Agricultural sponsorships can play a vital part in the income of a farm-area station, providing you create the proper kind of program for this sort of advertising.

Remember, too that with farm-oriented programming you have to consider when to schedule it. Farmers' work schedules must be taken into account, and these differ according to the type of farming done in your area.

Children's Programming

Children's programming has become an area of increasing concern in the television industry. One concern is the nature of entertainment programming, and the number and type of commercials contained within it. Another concern is the development of local programming of interest to children.

The major complaint about children's programming is that much of it is aimed at the "entertainment" of children and the selling of products, without regard to either the educational value of the programming or the appropriateness of the products sold.

In this area of programming critics point out that, all too often, television stations simply use a live host to provide transitions between cartoon segments and act as a pitch-person for commercials.

Spearheaded by Action for Children's Television (ACT), groups outside the broadcast industry have been exerting strong pressure for extensive reforms in children's programming. Ultimately, ACT wants to eliminate all commercials from children's programs and to require television stations to carry at least 14 hours of children's programming a week.

The industry has countered by limiting the types and number of commercials within children's programming. Efforts have been made to eliminate the practice of having the host sell products within the program.

ACT and the others have been particularly concerned about the advertising of food products which may have adverse nutritional or health effects, such as cereal with a great deal of sugar added. Other concerns have been with the manner in which toys are represented, and sale of vitamins within children's programming, the amount of violence depicted within children's viewing hours and, for some groups, the way in which women and minorities are depicted within children's programs. These groups feel that women are given stereotyped roles and that minorities are underrepresented or misrepresented.

What are the answers? The National Association of Broadcasters has moved towards stricter self-regulation limiting the number of commercial minutes within children's programs and restricting the role of program hosts as advertising salespersons.

The Federal Trade Commission has shown an interest in the nutritional value of foods and vitamins advertised.

Broadcasters have been working to improve the content and quality of children's programming. Some of the most significant advances have come from the group broadcasters, who have had the resources to produce their own children's programs for distribution to their stations and to other stations as syndicated programming.

The question of producing quality children's programming will continue to be a difficult one for individual broadcasters for some time to come. True, there has been an improvement in the quality of syndicated material available, but the most difficult task is raising the quality of local shows.

Basically, this means a greater investment in preparation, as well as in working cooperatively with community resources groups. These include colleges, school systems, consultants, parents groups, educational associations, and the local affiliates of some of the national organizations interested in children's programming. It also means being responsive to and seeking the advice of minority groups.

The group broadcasters have tackled the challenge by spending money—by pooling the resources of their stations to pay for consultants, top producers and, if necessary, location shooting. They are trying to pay back their costs by syndicating the programs.

The local station which wishes to improve its children's programming needs to see what sort of volunteer help it can recruit from the community. There are resources available, and probably what is needed more than anything else is to designate someone to produce and coordinate the local programming. Too often, local children's shows have been done on a wing and a prayer, with the host or hostess trying to produce the show while memorizing commercials. The director usually hasn't had time to do any more than develop the lineup for the day and make sure the props are available.

Remote Programs

Until recently the remote—away from the studio—broadcast was a big deal. It meant expensive preparations including ordering telephone lines and moving heavy equipment. Some major-market stations used bus-sized vehicles, just to handle their remote broadcasts.

Now the whole situation has changed. There as been such a miniaturization of equipment in recent years that both the capital investment and the amount or preparation needed to do a remote has been minimized.

The breakthrough is E-N-G—Electronic News Gathering. The equipment developed for live and videotape news coverage can just as well be used for remotes.

For most people in the industry, the technique is known as ENG. However, CBS News President Richard Salant preferred to call the technique E-C-C, for Electronic Camera Coverage. Salant's contention was that news coverage has not changed from a reportorial viewpoint; it's just that the camera is electronic, rather than mechanical (film).

The basic idea is this: The television camera has been miniaturized to the point that one person can easily carry the camera and its power supply. The signal from the camera can be relayed either by cable or miniature transmitter, to a small videotape recorder or to a microwave transmitter for relay back to the station.

The on-scene equipment needed for this sort of coverage can be installed in a half-ton panel truck or a good-sized station wagon. This compares very favorably with the 35 or 40-foot bus previously used for remotes.

While the electronic equipment package was developed primarily for news coverage, it has innumerable applications and is rapidly being applied to all kinds of programming situations.

Fig. 2-1. Electronic New Coordinator's console where incoming signals from ENG unit are viewed. Two-way radio communications permits editorial guidance to be relayed from the newsroom. (Photo courtesy of CBS Television Stations)

One station in North Carolina had been concerned about its inability to get out to the many small communities in its coverage area. Occasionally a film crew would break away to do some special filming, or the news department would be covering a hard news story, but these visits to the out-of-the-way communities were few and irregular. For the most part the station had to rely on inviting people from these communities to come into the city and appear on programs.

The station then purchased some of the new electronic equipment. Now the mobile unit can be driven out to a small community. A lightweight camera is set up, the miniaturized, videotape machine is turned on and the program material is recorded right on the scene.

The value of this operation is that it is quick, requires few personnel (usually two technicians and a reporter/producer) and is economical. Tape editing has become relatively easy, (Fig. 2-2) so that even if the original material is a little too long or too rough, it can be polished up quickly back at the studios (Fig. 2-3).

Most of the early programs using the equipment consisted of man-on-the-street interviews during which community residents discussed some of the issues that concerned them. However, there

Fig. 2-2. Editing console for electronic news gathering (ENG). Once the writer or producer selects scenes to be used from the rough tape, the portions selected for the final program can be assembled in the correct order using this console. (Photo courtesy of CBS Television Stations).

are many other ways to use the equipment. A local fair or agricultural feature could be taped. The mobile unit crew could visit craft groups or go to the high school.

These applications are rudimentary. But, with the type of equipment currently being installed in stations across the country, it is possible to do more involved remote programming (Fig. 2-4).

It would be no problem to do coverage of religious services from different churches, for instance. The remote truck can be driven up a half hour before the service, if need be. The service itself can be taped or, if the station has installed a microwave relay system, it can be beamed back to the studios for either live broadcast or taping for replay later (Fig. 2-5). Most of the current remote vans have only one camera because they have been set up for news coverage, but live program-type coverage could be done with a variable focus lens (Zoom lens) or by adapting the van for video mixing from more than one camera.

You could put on public forums throughout the area, by having a panel of experts answer questions from a studio audience. Visualize the possibilities for live or taped sports coverage! The same is true of parades and other public events. Once you have invested in the equipment, it's easy enough to utilize it for a wide array of programs.

You could take the ENG unit to the state or county fair—or if a congressional committee were holding a public hearing in your area, you might obtain permission to broadcast its sessions. How about live local drama performances at the high school or a college?

The new compact mobile units can give television stations opportunities for live and videotape programming, which were out of the question for all but a few major market stations in past years.

Documentaries

The new electronic equipment is being put to good use in the production of mini and maxi-documentaries. It's an inexpensive way

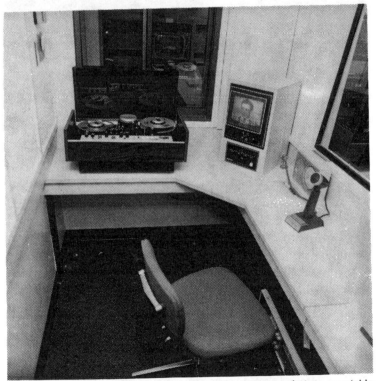

Fig. 2-3. Editing booth. A writer or producer can view tape shot on a portable videotape machine using tape playback machine, at left. A numerical counter beneath the TV monitor, center, is used to keep track of scenes. Editing decisions are written on a special form using the number on the numerical counter. An engineer assembles the finished tape using the number code on the editing decision form. (Photo courtesy of CBS Television Stations).

Fig. 2-4. Tape assembly room. Final tape is assembled here from rough tapes of interviews and other visuals. Console mentioned in Fig. 2-2 is at left of equipment seen here. (Photo courtesy of CBS Television Stations).

to do documentaries and some producers find the "live" quality enhances their programs.

The big cost saving is in the replacement of film by reuseable videotape. For remotes, the high cost of telephone lines can be eliminated.

Most stations which have equipped their news departments for ENG have found that it takes some time before they can produce documentaries on tape which compare with those done on film. The factors are training and experience. It takes a while for technicians, reporters, and producers to become familiar with the equipment. Particularly important is editing, which varies in ease and accuracy dependent on the skill of the editor and the type of equipment the station has installed. Generally it takes a little time before editors, new to videotape, can make tape edits which are reasonably close to the one-frame editing which is routine with film.

Also, most stations report it has taken a little while to sharpen camera operators' skills and to develop smooth production of what is called "double system" in film. This is when two, or even three sources of video (and audio, too) are combined into a finished product which may have visual changes while the audio track remains the same. For example, during an interview, the picture may dissolve to a scene of a location being discussed in audio portion of

Fig. 2-5. An ENG crew member aims a microwave dish at a receiver several miles away in order to transmit back to the station. (Photo courtesy of CBS Television Stations).

the interview. In film this is accomplished by editing and synchronizing two or more rolls of film and then projecting them on studio equipment where they are "mixed" and recorded on videotape.

The same effect can be accomplished with portable videotape, but it requires experience and the proper equipment. In some cases all the agony can be avoided just by changing the manner in which the story is shot.

The big advantage of tape is that it permits a producer to shoot liberal amounts of pictures and sound during the preparation of a documentary. A producer using film has to think about the high cost of the film stock and of processing it.

There is much debate on the relative quality of film and videotape products for documentary work. Some stations continue to insist that film is better for high quality work, while others mix film and tape according to what is best in each specific instance. Some stations are using only tape, and are working hard to upgrade their production to the high levels already accomplished by film documentary units.

One reason film has such a good reputation in documentary work is that it is usually possible to spend more time on lighting, framing and setting up during the production of a documentary. In day to day news coverage, too many shortcuts affect the quality of the film, which adversely are taken during shooting.

Basically, either medium works well in the hands of skilled, trained personnel who are given quality equipment.

Producers find videotape somewhat more convenient, because they are frequently permitted (by union contracts and available equipment) to go off to their offices and view the tape without having to wait for a film projector or a technician.

Oddly enough, the use of videotape for documentary production owes much of its development to educational broadcasters and independent producers who developed the techniques which are now being applied by commercial broadcasters. One development brought about by these early tape producers was the shooting of people and things in natural surroundings with natural sound. They avoided the artificiality associated with film in which lights are set up and the camera assigned a fixed position. The result was a loss of some visual and often a great deal of audio quality, but a whole new view of life was depicted. This technique is now common to both film and tape documentary work. Cameras have been taken off their fixed tripod positions and microphones have been opened to pick up ambient sound, as the camera operators move about among the people.

In Chapter 4 we will discuss at greater length how specific stations are applying the new electronic technology to their public affairs' programs.

Chapter 3
Practical Examples, Radio

In this and the following chapter we will discuss specific public affairs projects of radio and television stations. Some of our examples are stations which have received major national honors for the quality of their public affairs programming. While awards and honors are not an absolute test of quality, they are an effective way to pinpoint some examples of excellence, particularly since most organizations giving national awards rely on juries of acknowledged experts in making their selections.

You will find throughout this book repetitions of examples from certain stations. Some reappear because they have established their excellence in the public affairs field, others appear because the author had the opportunity of conducting in-depth, on-site interviews with their personnel.

The point to these case histories is that most stations can learn and adapt from these broadcasters. Most good ideas can be executed by large and small stations, after they have been tailored to match local conditions.

In addition, it is our hope that these examples will encourage you to develop new ideas of your own, and to aggressively seek recognition when you feel you have done an outstanding job.

WGMS

WGMS in Rockville, Maryland is primarily a classical music station. Traditionally stations programming this format, while noted for their excellence in musical taste, have operated with a minimal staff. Usually the focus was on the careful selection of music and the equally careful presentation of its on-air voices. News and public affairs have often taken second place in this sort of format.

WGMS has proven that a classical music station can attain national prominence in the public affairs area, while sticking to its main purpose, the presentation of serious music. The station was awarded the prestigious Peabody Award for its total programming effort, with specific attention to two projects: "200 Years of Music In America" and "Collector's Shelf."

"200 Years of Music in America" was produced in collaboration with outstanding music scholars from the Washington, D.C. area. It consisted of a 14-part history of American music. The series began with the pre-Colonial heritage from Europe and developed the history of American music through current theatrical and popular trends. Each program discussed and highlighted a different topic. Some of these included: "Fife, Drum and Bugle," "From Minstrelsy to Ives," "Sing, Sing, Sing," "Sousa to Fennell," "Music of the American City," "The Melting Pot," "Tapping Toes," and "The Great Rebels."

Each of the WGMS programs utilized two announcers and generally included up to 20 musical selections. The programs required about 20 minutes of scripted material, some of which was read over background music. The total length of each program was two hours.

"Collector's Shelf" was described by Eileen D. Curtis, the station's director of music and cultural affairs: "The show featured an unknown Hungarian pianist now eking out an existence on the West Coast whose prodigious gifts might be favorably compared with today's keyboard giants (such as Horowitz!). His tragic life story prevented him from gaining musical recognition. This program presented him in a rare recital, which I believe was a spur-of-the-moment concert."

As you can see, WGMS was recognized for doing what it always does, presenting fine arts programming; only in these cases the station put extra effort into doing unique programs, which the Peabody judges noted.

Their relevancy to public affairs? That's partly determined by your definition of community—in this case the community was more intellectual and cultural, than geographical. The technique is applicable—doing what your format dictates in the best way possible.

What makes this illustration particularly interesting is that prior to the production of these series, a major fire had destroyed the WGMS studios and so all production and programming had to be done, using available equipment, from an old transmitter building. Obviously you do not need posh surroundings and the finest equipment to do a good job, if your script and content are good.

Some of the other public affairs programming at WGMS includes "Soul of the Classics," in which the station's community affairs director plays and talks about music by black composers and discusses the work of black artists. Another program, which the station syndicated to other stations in the RKO chain was "Heritage" which discussed the roots of minority groups.

WCBS

WCBS is the flagship station for the CBS-owned radio stations. This big-market, all-news station, located in New York City, has won a truckload of awards for its outstanding public affairs efforts.

One of its outstanding efforts was a six-week series of special reports entitled: "The Criminal Justice System."

One of the techniques used by WCBS reporter Jerry Nachman, was to follow police officers and defendants through the criminal justice system, step by step.

Nachman interviewed the people involved in each step of the judicial process. They included arresting officers, desk sergeants, the suspects, attorneys and other key individuals. As much of the tape as possible was obtained while activities were taking place, such as the original booking and search of a suspect.

The series followed the criminal justice chain, featuring sections titled: *Arrests, Jail or Bail?, To Plea or Not To Plea, Who Goes to Prison?* and *Juvenile Criminals.*

There was no set pattern to Nachman's approach. He looked for strong tape, doing on-scene taping where possible, but the majority of the programs features comments by the people who oversee the criminal justice system in New York State. Some programs featured only one interviewee, others had as many as five voices. Some of the individuals interviewed appeared only once; others were used in more than one program.

This particular series illustrates good integration of a station's public affairs efforts. The six weeks of programming were structured as follows: each week featured five separate mini-documentaries which were aired six times daily, one segment each weekday. At the end of the week the five reports were compiled into a 13-minute program, which has aired twice each on Saturday and Sunday. On Friday morning the station broadcast a live 55-minute call-in, panel segment during which experts discussed the week's topic. This was repeated on tape later in the day.

This is an outstanding example of skilled use of public affairs time to gain maximum audience. The secret to the production of the program lies in the expertise of the reporter-producer who has specialized in criminal justice matters for a number of years.

WCBS follows a consistent policy of preparing editorials to voice specific opinions on topics covered by public affairs programming. In the case of a series such as the one we have just described, the station would take a stand on improvements it felt should be made in the criminal justice system.

WCBS does many other interesting public affairs programs. One unusual effort had two applications. The station conducted a series of "Stop Smoking Clinics" and later followed with the "WCBS Diet Clinic." Both series were prepared in conjunction with a known regimen for the cessation of smoking and the loss of weight. A series of warm-up features were run to arouse interest and get listeners to write in for a free kit of instructional materials, which helped them participate in the clinic. The clinics themselves were done in daily stages, with a specific regimen and set of goals announced each day. In addition, a station reporter interviewed a counselor during each stage of the regimen, and hosted question and answer sessions during which the public could call in. The "Diet Clinic" ran ten weeks. Obviously, long-running series like these have potential for reinforcing listening habits—an excellent fringe benefit for the station.

WRFM

WRFM is a very successful FM-only good music station in New York City. One of the programs for which the station has honored was "Crime in the Streets." Former Community Affairs Director Murray Roberts explained why WRFM got involved in the project. He said: "We were reaching the point where the juvenile crime problem had become so serious that people were literally afraid to walk the streets... When I decided to do this, I felt that the contrast between those that were doing...young kids...and...the victims ...the elderly...made an interesting contrast. And I also felt that it would provide a perfect opportunity to describe the inadequacies of the juvenile court system, and the reasons why it was so difficult to actually get kids who were committing these crimes off the streets to where they could receive any sort of help at all."

Roberts got important assistance from a special unit of the New York City Police Department which deals with crime against the elderly. He interviewed many of the elderly who had been the victims of crime. And Roberts was fortunate enough to talk with a few of the juveniles who had been involved in crimes against the elderly.

Roberts recounted one experience: "One of them was a killer ...It seemed to be terribly right to him to be doing what he was doing, even to the point of killing someone...and all because somebody had ripped him off for something like a hundred dollars..."

Roberts added: "The other interesting thing...was the fact that here we have a system that thought that it had rehabilitated a kid. He had been found guilty (of course, as a juvenile you don't go to jail for that)...was sentenced for 18 months to a juvenile house, after ten months was brought back down to one of the weekend residences, admitted previously to killing somebody else...didn't get caught on that one—and the system thought that this kid was rehabilitated."

Roberts went on: "When you asked him...'You're not going to be 17 or 18...and you know if you were to go out and kill someone now...you're going to be a felon, you're going to be part of the criminal court system,...would you do something like that again?' 'Oh, yeah, if that's my justice I'd go ahead and do the same thing.' And that's somebody we thought was rehabilitated!"

This is why the radio documentary is so effective is that it uses voices of real people to tell an important story.

WRFM went beyond simply pointing out that a juvenile crime problem existed. The station tried to get information across to the elderly on how they could protect themselves and offered suggestions on places they could call for additional help.

One way WRFM extends the effectiveness of its public affairs programs is by offering the station as a resource. For instance, if a booklet of interest to the public is available, the station obtains copies and distributes them. Some of the publications which have been sent to listeners include booklets on divorce laws, stress and alcoholism.

WRFM uses the mini-documentary approach for its public affairs programs, because it is basically a wall-to-wall (all) music station and feels that talk segments should not exceed three or three and one-half minutes.

Roberts, who is now connected with a non-profit organization, says his station—which did not editorialize—would permit a mini-documentary to take a strong editorial stand.

Roberts explained: "We went in with the idea that a documentary has some sort of bias or slant... we do take positions, and the tag ends of each of our programs say 'if there are contrasting points of view you know, we'll welcome them."

Roberts recalled only two instances, during his 7-year tenure as the station's community affairs director, when requests came in seeking to add to the information contained in a mini-documentary. He feels that this indicates that the station had presented all the major points of view in its various series.

WVOX

WVOX in the suburban New York county of Westchester has been honored a number of times for its intense community involvement. Led by dynamic Bill O'Shaughnessy, the station does things which, on the surface, appear outrageous.

O'Shaughnessy recalled preparations for the 1976 Bicentennial Fourth of July weekend. It was "...a special program ...playing patriotic music for three straight days and reading the Constitution, once an hour, or the Bill of Rights. John Philip Sousa, it's an out and out, no-holds-barred, knock-down-drag-out, no apologies to anybody, true blue patriotic program."

O'Shaughnessy prides himself on being able to meet community needs with his flexible programming. In an interview he said: "A kid came in the other day and wanted to raise money for the community action program. They lost all their funds so we had an all-day broadcast here, had Pearl Primus the dancer and all the greats, Ossie Davis and Rosie Greer came down, took over the damn radio station. It was so crowded here that here was some...youngster over there sitting behind my desk...eating a tuna fish sandwich."

WVOX has received most of its plaudits for all-around public affairs efforts, including it's self-styled town reports. O'Shaughnessy says: "There's a lot of news stories which are not hard news and which are not memo-pad or public service items, there's an area in between there and we do that on a daily basis."

Localism is the by-word at WVOX. "The classic mistake of a station our size is to try and be regional," said O'Shaughnessy.

Not all religion on WVOX is relegated to Sunday morning. O'Shaugnessy described one religious program: "We're running it not at six o'clock in the morning, we're running it at noon on Saturday. The program itself is simple, you get a different clergyman...different styles. You get a marvelous old Irish monsignor sitting there with (a local black minister) with his big diamond ring, and its marvelous. They talk about church life, and religion in Westchester and religion in America. The first part of the program concerns church notes and then there's a discussion of religious topics."

WVOX tries to be flexible. "A guy called me the other day," said O'Shaughnessy, "...to do a thing on Jewish patriots during the Bicentennial...so we made a series out of it, five 15-minute programs."

And yet another example: "I remember the Vietnam protesters ...moratorium day. We did an open line all day...this really was a platform, a forum...."

Oddly enough, WVOX is not strictly a talk station. It's mainstay is still the disc jockey-playing middle-of-the-road music. However, the program schedule is a jumble of talk segments, features, music, news, sports and call-in shows. O'Shaughnessy calls his station's format "community radio." His programming philosophy is simply to dig out the kinds of programming needs that exist in his coverage area and to respond to these needs. As a result the station is a potpourri of ethnic programs, town reports, community reports—

such as one originating from the giant Co-op City housing complex in New York City's North Bronx—sports, local news and talk show.

WRKL

Another suburban New York station which responds to the needs of its audience is WRKL in Mt. Ida, Rockland County. Rockland is a middle-class bedroom county for people who work in New York City. Long before the commuters came from the city, Rockland had been an agricultural county, with farmers sharing space with a few wealthy estate owners and a scattering of artists and writers who had fled Greenwich Village.

Today Rockland county is bulging with new homes, condominiums, new schools, tax problems and big mortgages. The needs of its residents are different from those of residents of nearby New York City. And enough miles separates Rockland from New York that the big metropolitan stations are unable to give the county intensive daily news and public affairs coverage.

Thus WRKL, a 1,000-watt daylighter, tries to fill these special needs. The station has been honored a number of times for the excellence of its local programming, which is done with the most stringent budgetary limitations.

Mrs. Betty Ramey owns WRKL, and she has a clearcut philosophy regarding the station's role. "The only reason," said Mrs. Ramey, "for suburban radio, as I see it, is that it serves the community in some way in which city radio cannot. City radio cannot afford to cover Rockland County news and public affairs. So we cover everything that happens in Rockland, thereby giving people something which, for them, will perhaps outdistance New York radio in importance, and, when it does, they all wake up and turn the station on."

We have spoken earlier of WRKL's noontime, call-in, telephone-talk show, which is a cornerstone of the station's public affairs' effort. Other public affairs programs include "Another View," devoted to the problems of Rockland County's black community. It is moderated by a black school teacher and features interviews with community leaders. There are also local religious programs, scheduled on Sunday.

The station joined with the Rockland Historical Society in co-producing a series of historical vignettes. As Mrs. Ramey said:

"They produced them in writing, we produced them on the air." It's an example of a small local station making use of local resources to expand the scope and quality of its programming. Most communities have the technical expertise to produce programs of this sort, all that is usually needed is the production expertise of the station to develop the available information into a radio program.

KKUA

KKUA is located in Honolulu, Hawaii. The island state presents a number of challenges to broadcasters, including serving the state's diverse ethnic constituencies.

According to Public Service Director Karen King: "Undoubtedly the most interesting program unique to our station and Hawaii is a religious program produced by the Waikiki Beach Chaplaincy entitled "Soul Talk." Waikiki Chaplain Bob Turnbill hosts the program featuring local talent, letters from listeners, and 'rap' on today's problems and solutions by young people everywhere. "Soul Talk" is aired twice each Sunday.

The station also airs a nightly mixture of news and public affairs which includes in-depth stories, unusual happenings and interesting information which would be overlooked in regular newscasts.

WBLX

WBLX is an FM-station in Mobile, Alabama. The format features contemporary music. How does a station in a highly-competitive market, like Mobile, meet its public affairs obligations? Here are some examples:

WBLX airs a five-minute report by the mayor of Mobile each day, Monday through Saturday at 10:55 a.m. For the most part it deals with actions taken by the city council and municipal leaders.

On Sunday afternoons, the station airs a series of public affairs programs: At 2:05, right after the news, WBLX broadcasts "Altogether Mobile." The program's theme is health and education and it is done in conjunction with Bishop State Junior College. Generally the format consists of a discussion.

At 2:30, the station airs "Opinion," a 30-minute interview with a significant guest. The station's public affairs director interviews the guest on local and regional issues.

At 3 o'clock, WBLX airs "Problems in the Community." The news director and three panelists do a "Face the Nation" type program, interviewing one guest on a leading issue in the news.

WBLX concentrates on music programming. However, the station's concern for public affairs programming is indicated by the fact that General Manager Larry Williams employs both a community affairs director and a full-time person who works on public affairs programming.

The subjects of the interviews are developed through the station's ascertainment program, which helps top management define the important issues in their service area.

Next, we move on to television public affairs programming.

Chapter 4
Practical Examples, Television

This chapter is devoted to examples of public affairs programs aired on television stations. As in the preceding chapter, some examples have been gathered through contacts with stations which have been honored with distinguished national prizes. Other examples are the result of on-scene interviews at some randomly selected stations. The latter category is included because some stations place a great deal of emphasis on winning prizes, while others concentrate more on discharging their public affairs obligations as part of their total activities.

Television public affairs directors have to think in terms of total programs rather than mini-programs to fit into their schedules. There are also technical complications to television and there are always budgetary concerns, especially when one embarks on a documentary.

The basic tools in television public affairs programs are half-hour and hour programs, interviews (within other types of programming) and mini-documentaries which usually run in the news.

Inevitably the public compares television public affairs programs to the entertainment programming which makes up the greater part of the station's schedule. So the public affairs director is faced with having to make the programs interesting without overspending. The matter of audience interest becomes critical when you plan a documentary for prime time evening viewing.

And you can't neglect your public affairs obligation in television with a three-minute feature slipped in between two records. So you are dealing in half hours and hours; and there is tremendous pressure to make certain that you don't deplete the station's audience during a public affairs program, especially if the program has been assigned to a prime time.

The object is to make the program interesting. Approach this problem by choosing an interesting topic and by using interesting people, good production and visualization—after all television is pictures. That's what people watch.

Visualization becomes more difficult and more expensive when you move to documentaries or on-location programs. But the investment in on-scene film or tape can be well worth it in the final quality of the program. It doesn't make sense, in many cases, to have a bunch of people sitting around in a studio discussing the problems of welfare mothers when you can go out and visit their homes, talk with recipients, go where they shop, get medical care, schooling and training—and thus visualize their plight.

Public affairs programs should respond to the needs of the community. In the chapter which follows we will go into detail about ascertainment. Most television stations now key their public affairs programs to the ideas they develop in their ascertainment program.

Next, we will look at how some actual stations program their public affairs time.

WFSB-TV

WFSB Television in Hartford, Connecticut is a CBS affiliate. The station, which has a long history in the community under former ownership and call letters, is currently owned by the Post-Newsweek chain of broadcast stations, newspapers and magazines.

The present management makes a vigorous effort to be responsive and to do a good job in public affairs programming, since they purchased a property with a long history of local involvement.

WFSB produced two prime time, magazine shows a week. One called "Land of the Three" and has been described as a local, half-hour version of the popular CBS News public affairs' program, "60 Minutes."

According to the station's Vice President for Public Affairs, Richard F. Ahles, "Land of the Three" contains three or four story segments a week.

Ahles described one of the segments of which he was particularly proud: It…"was a story about how the Congress of Racial Equality was high-pressuring small businessmen into giving, buying ads in publications of dubious value…. It was a tough one to do," said Ahles, "because we got all kinds of pressure from CORE not to do the story, all kinds of telephone calls threatening us with terrible things, but we did it anyway; it was right."

On the lighter side, "Land of the Three" visited a shop which sells very expensive junk.

Ahles recalls another feature: "At election time we went to one of the smallest towns…where, the last time, the first selectman lost by one vote; so we did a pre-election story and then went out election night to cover it."

The weekend anchorperson, who works for the public affairs department three days a week, acts as host for the "Land of the Three" program. In addition, Ahles has two full-time reporters, one of whom is also a producer. He also has a full-time photographer and sound technician, plus various other technicians as the need arises. The department is rounded out by a production assistant-secretary. The hostess for a women's show also contributes magazine segments from time to time.

The other prime time magazine format was called "Getting Down to Business." It featured some substantial segments on business topics plus related briefs. Some topics covered by the program include the arms industry in Connecticut, the insurance industry and its reluctance to provide coverage for the swine flu innoculation program, and an essay on executive dining rooms.

Occasionally WFSB likes to devote a whole week to a topic and schedule a coordinated, saturated series of programs, mini-documentaries and editorials on the subject.

Related interviews are scheduled on the morning interview program.

One such topic was the public schools. WFSB aired several programs on various aspects of the public schools, including an hour just on the financing of public education. The news department did a series during the same week on vandalism in the schools, as its part of the station's overall saturation approach to the the topic.

Another saturation week dealt with crime. A major program in the series was called "The Chair." It dealt with capital punishment, which Connecticut had abolished, but which was under reconsideration by the U.S. Supreme Court. The public affairs department traced down a man who had been waiting on death row when the state did away with capital punishment. The convict subsequently escaped and was later arrested in Massachusetts for another crime. WFSB interviewed him in a Massachusetts prison and he recounted his experiences and feelings during that long wait on death row.

The total package consists of documentary specials, mini-documentaries in the news, possibly segments on the magazine shows and interviews on the daily interview program. All this integrated programming is topped off with editorials on related matters. This approach is designed to allow in-depth coverage of more complicated and sophisticated problems—topics which can't be adequately covered in a one-shot special.

Dick Ahles described some of the other programs schedule during "Crime Week." One dealt with women in crime. Another was called "Up Against the Wall." Ahles said: "Five years ago there was a big criminal justice system conference...and they brought together judges and prosecutors and cops and wardens and convicts and everybody who is involved in the criminal justice system.... They made a lot of recommendations to reform the criminal justice system in Connecticut.

"Well, we took about 20 minutes of that film, that we had done back then, and we brought in five of the participants and said, 'Well, what's happened since then, and why not?'... A lawyer, who complained five years ago that judges just didn't even give a damn and weren't even participating in this conference...well, he's a judge now, and we showed him saying that and...he said 'well, I've moderated my position a bit." Recalled Ahles: "The best thing we ever did, I guess, was a show called "The Nine-Year-Old in Norfolk Prison." This was about a 28-year-old retarded man with a nine-year old mentality who was convicted of murder in Springfield (Massachusetts) on very, very dubious evidence. And I think we raised enough doubts about it that well, he did get a new trial and his conviction was set aside by the Massachusetts Supreme Court. This program did it.... I mean that doesn't happen very often."

According to the WFSB public affairs director, the main source of the station's public affairs ideas is the ascertainment process.

Ahles said a program on problems involving ambulance service in Hartford was done as the result of complaints from members of the public. The program won an Ohio State Award.

WFSB airs a weekly, locally-produced, religious program called "My Neighbor's Religion," which, as Ahles said, "deals with the lesser known religious groups that don't fit into this nice comfortable Protestant, Catholic, Jewish mold."

WFSB also originates a religious series called "We Believe" which is rotated among the three major faiths.

Ahles said his station covers religion in other ways. "On the magazine show," Ahles said, "I cover religious topics very frequently...I do believe that covering religion in public affairs is important—and not just (by) segregating it to the Sunday morning spots."

Various colleges and universities lend their cooperation to a series called "From the College Campus," which is aired on Sunday morning. And, like many, many other stations WFSB has its own Sunday news interview show, called "Face the State."

WXII-TV

WXII-TV is located in Winston-Salem, North Carolina. The Channel 12 facility serves a three-city market made up of Winston-Salem, High Point and Greensboro.

WXII's staple item is a weekday hour-long morning program which is primarily devoted to public affairs. It includes two short newscasts. During the newscasts a translator appears on the screen for the benefit of deaf viewers.

From time to time, members of the audience are invited to call in and ask questions of persons being interviewed.

A regularly scheduled public affairs program is "Close Up" which deals with an issue or problem confronting communities within the viewing area. For instance, the program might focus on health care, which is a major concern, especially in rural areas of North Carolina.

WXII uses the mini-documentary format to cover some topics and full-length documentaries to cover others. Sometimes "Close-Up"—which is primarily a studio interview show—becomes a film documentary.

A series of programs dealing with North Carolina's history during the nation's founding years was so well received, it was rebroadcast on the state educational television network.

Many stations do major prime time documentaries in response to specific local concerns. During a recent economic downturn in the textile and furniture industries—important to North Carolina's economy—WXII did a one-hour special involving interviews with both corporate heads and workers with the aim of demonstrating the economic viability of the area.

WCBB-TV

WCBB-TV is an educational station located in Lewiston, Maine. It is operated under the auspices of three small colleges: Colby, Bates and Bowdoin.

Inherently, educational stations air a great deal of public affairs programming. The main point to the inclusion of an educational station among our examples is to point out some of the different approaches which can be taken with public affairs programs. We selected WCBB to point out that there are programs in production that do not exceed the resources of even the most carefully-budgeted commercial station.

WCBB is not one of the nation's well-endowed educational stations. In fact, the station still uses black and white studio cameras. But some of the programming is different and interesting, and illustrates that such programs can be produced on a minimal budget.

A program designed specifically to suit the nature of the market is called "Up Country." It is a Maine program—about the state and aimed at a native audience. The station goes out with its mobile unit—an old bus—and tapes events such as a log roll on the Kennebec River or salmon fishing on the Androscoggin River.

The program's host is the head of the state Audubon Society, and the topics deal primarily with the natural wonders of Maine.

A four-part series called "Home" dealt with housing conditions, fair housing laws, different types of structures and federal housing regulations. Housing is a major concern in Maine where a low median income and a severe climate create housing problems for many families.

"Maine Medical Call" is patterned along the line of a similar program originated by a commercial station in Boston. The WCBB program features a doctor in the studio who takes calls from viewers on the week's medical topic. Frequently he is assisted by other specialists who answer audience questions.

Each week WCBB airs "Maine Week," which brings together journalists from south and central Maine to discuss the major issues being talked about in the state. The program also deals in how the press covers these issues.

And "Back Stage" provides an outlet for cultural features, folk music performances, little theatre and craft demonstrations. On occasion the mobile unit is sent out to tape features for this program.

While WCBB makes frequent use of its old mobile unit, the actual program production is very straightforward, because there are not enough personnel available to do a great deal of editing. Most shows are taped as live performances from top to bottom.

Programming Director Michael Mears said one of his station's most popular programs was a simple quiz show, called "So You Think You Know Maine". The guests answer questions about their state including its long history and heritage. The winners are given token prizes—such as a chicken or a box of bricks—but the program draws large audiences for its tried and true format.

WSBK-TV

WSBK is a UHF independent station on Channel 38 and is located in Boston. The station is run with a close eye on its budget, since the mixed market is dominated by three commercial VHF's, an educational VHF and has access to at least four other VHF signals. This means that a UHF independent must program skillfully and economically, in order to gain the needed audience and also discharge its public service obligation.

The mainstay of WSBK's public affairs programming was "The Tom Larson Show," named for the program's host. It was aired from 10 to 11 a.m., Monday through Friday and, according to Program Manager Richard Beach, tried for controversial guests. Beach said: "It sticks pretty much to the topics that our ascertainment surveys show are the problems." The program can have one, two or three guests, depending on the nature of the topic and the public interest in the guest.

WSBK deals with an independent producer for the production of the station's half-hour weekly black-oriented program, called "The Drum Show." It uses the interview format, with the producer acting as host. Beach said the station maintains close control over the program and has, on occasion, refused to air segments which did not meet its standards. The station management provides guest and topic input to the outside producer, who is responsible for rounding up guests and subjects for the weekly program.

Channel 38 also produced a weekly religion program in conjunction with the Massachusetts Council of Rabbis.

WSBK does not have a news department. This means the station lacks the basic equipment and personnel to do documentaries. Beach solved the problem by assigning each of the station's four producer-directors a documentary. The producers shoot their own film using the station's one sound-on-film camera (Fig. 4-1). The exposed film is processed by a commercial laboratory and the editing is done at the studios. The station has remote facilities, but these are designed, specifically, for live sports' coverage which is one of the mainstays of the station's programming. The units are not well suited to documentary production, nor are they available at convenient times.

Documentaries have included essays on life in Boston and a program specifically dealing with problems facing women. Production is spaced over a considerable length of time because the producers work on their documentaries during lulls in their other duties.

WGAN-TV

WGAN Television is located in Portland, Maine. The CBS affiliate serves south and central Maine and portions of New Hampshire.

While the station operates from a strong economic base as a combined AM-FM-TV facility, co-owned with newspapers, the area's troubled economy demands careful attention to budgets.

WGAN-TV follows the almost universal pattern of airing a new conference type program, this one called "At Issue." It is normally a

Fig. 4-1. Typical 16mm sound-on-film (SOF) camera used for news and documentary work. (Photo courtesy of Cinema Products Corp.)

half-hour but can be expanded to an hour if the issue or guest warrants. The program, according to WGAN's Vice-President and General Manager Charles Sanford, makes a point of trying to look at the future. It focuses on an issue which may become significant in the weeks ahead, rather than taking a retrospective look at the news.

Outside reporters from all media are invited to participate, based on their specialities.

An unusual public affairs feature is the "Main Opinion Poll" which runs three times a week on television. Sanford said the results of the poll are frequently similar to results received from scientifically-designed opinion polls covering the same topics.

WGAN-TV has a regular rotation of clerics from different faiths who come in to record half-hour programs, which are primarily musical in format.

Sanford said he had become concerned that the station wasn't doing enough in the documentary area. His solution was to assign each news department reporter a specific month for which he or she would produce a documentary. The reporter would pick the issue in conjunction with the news director, and then produce the program. Sanford said this would guarantee a minimum of 12 scheduled documentaries a year. In addition, the station does specials as specific situations demand, such as the "red tide" which periodically fouls the fishing and recreational waters along the Maine coastline.

During the 1976 election season the station worked with the League of Women Voters to produce debate programs featuring the congressional candidates.

DOCUMENTARIES

Documentaries are the showcase public affairs programming for most television stations. Stations take their film and tape cameras out into their communities, catching slices of life and talking with people about important local issues. Because television is a dramatic and visual medium, a well-produced documentary can have a powerful impact, both on the individual viewer and on the total audience.

Because documentaries can be showcase efforts, some stations are able to sell them to prestige advertisers who want their messages framed by special programming.

Each year literally hundreds of television documentaries are produced by local stations. We are citing a few examples here to demonstrate the diversity of programs which can be produced, and to point out that the big city conglomerate-owned stations do not have a monopoly on good programming.

Our first example is a program produced by an ABC affiliate in Jonesboro, Arkansas.

KAIT-TV

It took News Director Jack Hil four months to produce "Behind These Bars," a documentary on county jails in northeast Arkansas. Following the airing of the program, a committee was designated by the county grand jury to investigate the feasibility of constructing a new jail.

Hill said: "I got the idea because of proposed minimum jail standards that were to go into effect in Arkansas and through my own observation of county jail conditions in our area. I probably had the idea in the back of my head for 9 or 10 months. During that time I collected whatever clippings I found in local newspapers. That gave me some leads when I began work on the project in earnest...the leg work was done primarily on the phone. I spent hours and hours on calls with anyone I could think of who might have some information that might be useful."

Hill outlined a 7-part series which was run in mini-documentary form on the station's 6 and 10 p.m. news programs and then, combined, as a half-hour special.

Hill and a cameraman did the interviewing and filming. The project involved six out of town trips, which would be a strain on the any small market news department.

As to reaction, Hill reported: "A grand jury met in the county we covered with two jails, both condemned. They're looking into ways to improve county jail conditions. The talk is of a new, centrally-located jail. We're told by county residents our reporting was a definite factor in their starting to do something. It was the first time, apparently, any real steps have been taken to improve the jails."

WGN-TV

WGN Television in Chicago is one of the nation's powerhouse stations. Producer Forrest H. Respess produced a documentary entitled "Grant Me The Courage," which dealt with alcoholic rehabilitation.

The idea began in an unusual manner. A WGN reporter, John Hogan, had covered stories on the opening of the Alcoholic Rehabilitation Center at Lutheran General Hospital in Park Ridge, Illinois during the late 1960s. Midway through 1973 the reporter suggested to his news director that the center's program might be a fitting topic for a documentary, and Respess was assigned to produce the program.

Respess recalled: "We had our first meeting with the administrators of the center.... Understandably, some of the Center personnel had early objections to our proposal. However, when we convinced them that our sole intention was to show what could be done for the alcoholic...and not hold him up to ridicule...we were given the green light to proceed. Inasmuch as many news stories and documentaries on alcoholism had to resort to the distorted voice and darkened profile, it was my desire to do our program without restrictions."

For two months the WGN crew spent hours at the Center, sitting in on and, in some cases, participating in counseling sessions, group therapy meetings and other functions.

"It was imperative," said Respess, "that all of the patients accept us and get used to our presence. Consequently, the four of us on the crew spent full time at the Center before shooting any film.

"We insisted that there be no 'staging' and that everything filmed would be the same as if we weren't there. It was obvious from the beginning that we would have to shoot with available light only." This presented many problems having to do with mixtures of interior lighting fixtures and day-to-day variations in the outside light.

Respess added: "We used a 'shotgun' microphone so that none of the counselors or patients would be restricted by having to wear a microphone. The Center is in direct line with a landing approach to O'Hare Airport, which negated use of wireless mics.

"Our biggest concern was finding a patient who would give us permission to follow him through the three-week program. As it turned out, we had two primary patients to follow...a 33-year-old factory worker from Peoria, and a 40-year-old suburban housewife. In addition, 14 other patients agreed to be photographed without restriction. All of the patients, plus members of their families, who agreed to participate, signed a release drawn up by attorneys for both WGN Continental Broadcasting and Lutheran General Hospital."

What Respess' employer and the hospital were concerned about was being accused of either invading the privacy of or defaming the character of the patients or their families. This is why they obtained releases—a common practice in documentary work.

Respess said: "In order to keep a low profile, many times our cameraman would be crunched in the corner during a counseling session, with the microphone stuck in a wastebasket and the cables running under the door.

"The only times we had to resort to a distorted image was during the filming of Alcoholics Anonymous and Al-Anon meetings. This was done to protect the anonymity of the speakers who talked to the patients and the patients' families.

"We completed the three weeks of filming without any serious problems. In all, we shot some 29,000 feet of film for the one-hour documentary. The editing took about three and a half weeks and about 25 hours to transfer the film to videotape."

"Grant Me The Courage" was aired in mid-1975 and has been an award winner.

WCKT-TV

WCKT Television, the NBC affiliate in Miami may be the nation's "winningest" television station. It has won—and won again—virtually every honor bestowed on television stations for public affairs programming.

To bear out this point, here's an excerpt from some correspondence with News Director Gene Strul: "This year," said Strul, "we have won, to date, the George Foster Peabody, SDX, National Headliner, Robert F. Kennedy Journalism Memorial Foundation, Scripps Howard Foundation, Freedoms Foundation and three Broadcast Industry Media Awards." That's a lot for a portion of one year. (We will talk in some detail about winning awards in Chapter 10. You will also find in the same chapter a list of some of the major awards.)

The long list of awards won by WCKT points to two facts—the excellence of the programs, and the aggressive and knowledgeable pursuit of awards which must have taken place.

A good part of winning is knowing what awards are around, who gives them for what and then matching up your own efforts with the specifications for pertinent awards.

To cite one documentary effort by WCKT as described by Strul: "...the origin was a medical doctor who reported to us that two of his patients had decided against abortions as proposed by an abortion clinic. Following examination, he advised them they were not pregnant in the first place, hence, our investigative series. It has resulted in six arrests and promised legislation."

WCKT, a major station in a major market, specializes in solid investigative journalism and has the personnel and money to do a well-produced, in-depth job.

WTTG-TV

WTTG is a VHF independent in Washington, D.C. The station has built a reputation over the years for its 10 p.m. news, which follows the major early news but preceeds the traditional 11 o'clock newscasts on the three network affiliated stations.

A tip to a producer led to several exclusives on a major scandal involving the purchasing of meat for use by the military.

Producer Joel Seidman credits good contacts on Capitol Hill and a series of "leaks"—information given him intentionally and confidentially by various sources—for providing the information needed to put together a series of two-minute mini-documentaries on the scandal, which were aired on the company's stations in five major markets.

A passing remark overheard at Andrews Air Force Base led Seidman to check a source at the Senate Government Operations Subcommittee. He learned that senators and committee staff members were conducting an inspection of a shipment of meat purchased by the military the following day. Seidman managed to contact a meat packer who had been the source of the original complaint which set the committee into action.

The following day the WTTG crew showed up and after a combination of negotiating and muscle, were allowed to film the inspection process, which revealed that nearly the whole shipment failed an inspection by experts flown in for the occasion. In addition pieces of insects and clumps of animal hair were found in the samples.

The station aired reports regularly, and eventually, hearings were held on Capitol Hill. Among the illegal acts uncovered were instances of bidding competition by firms owned by the same individuals, and bribes given to meat inspectors.

It was a blockbuster project, yet it resulted from a few chance remarks overheard at lunch.

CHILDREN'S PROGRAMS

Programs oriented towards children have become a major concern to groups outside the broadcast industry. The major contentions, as we pointed out earlier, have to do with the type of material included within these programs and its potential effect on children. Critics feel that many children's programs are dominated by violence, racial and sexual stereotypes, and excess commercialism.

The broadcasting industry is responding to these criticisms by policing the number and type of commercials placed in children's programs and by improving the educational and instructive qualities of the programs.

Some examples of children's programming, devised with these criticisms in mind: "Marshall Efron's Illustrated, Simplified and Painless Sunday School" which was developed by CBS News to provide a creative introduction to Biblical stories.

"Hot Fudge," devised by WXYZ-TV in Detroit to promote preventive medicine in the field of mental health.

KLRN Television in Austin, Texas approached a problem particular to its market by devising "Carascolendas" a bilingual, bicultural program for English and Spanish speaking children.

The Post-Newsweek Group of stations produced "The Reading Show" which combined print materials with their broadcasts in an effort to improve reading comprehension and vocabulary among elementary school children. The group's stations coordinated the venture with school systems in their respective markets.

"Call It Macaroni"

In order to illustrate, in depth, the type of programming that is being developed for children, we have selected a program series, "Call It Macaroni," produced by the Westinghouse Broadcasting Company.

George E. Moynihan, a WBC vice-president, was the executive producer for the series. He explained how the project got started: "We felt there was very little programming being done for young people except for cartoons and programs of that nature...we felt there was a very real need, particularly within commercial television, for programming for, roughly, the 8 to 12-year-old youngster..."

Previously, two Westinghouse stations had tried formats which involved taking children on trips and letting the children describe the trip themselves. It occurred to the Westinghouse programmers that perhaps this idea could be developed.

Next Westinghouse did extensive research, including seeking advice from leading groups interested in children's programming and from experienced producers. A guidebook was developed; and everyone who was interviewed for potential employment on the project was asked to become familiar with the guidebook before the

Fig. 4-2. Learning all about dolphins from trainer Kathy Krieger, left, and the dolphins themselves—Samba and Damon—are Jeff Hawkinson and Sandy Schiller, of Stamford, Conn. The youngsters' experiences with dolphins and other creatures, including killer whales, at the Miami Sequarium are shown on the "Call It Macaroni" special, "Some of My Best Friends Are Dolphins." (Photo courtesy of Group W. Productions).

discussions commenced. As a result, the originators of the "Macaroni" series started out with a common set of objectives.

A small production unit was formed, with Moynihan supervising. The unit consisted of two producers and a cameraman. The Westinghouse stations were asked to provide an associate producer, and when needed, personnel, and film editors.

Moynihan elaborated on the organization: "It gave us the necessary manpower to supplement our small group. It also gave us some people to help us start lining up kids in, at least, our own markets. And…it gave the people at our local stations an excellent training area. We had each of our stations speak with schools and other youth organizations in our five markets."

Moynihan continued: "They probably pulled together two or three or four hundred kids in each of those markets, and then the producers went…and spoke to all of those kids…and (got) that group down to, I would guess, a basic pool of some 15 kids…from which they used two or three at a time, usually three per program." (Fig. 4-2).

The Westinghouse executive described a typical program: "We took three kids from Philadelphia...to Mount Hood.... They climbed Mount Hood.

"In each case we take kids from one environment and plunge them into a totally foreign environment and totally foreign activity.

"There were three kids from Pittsburgh," said Moynihan, "who went to join a traveling circus in the Rocky Mountains. They had never been out of Pittsburgh, never mind having had anything to do with a circus, and yet, before that week was over, one of them actually flew on the trapeze. Another one, a young girl, took part in a human pyramid, with a group of tumblers from Algiers; and the third youngster served as the barker, master of ceremonies."

"The basic thing," Moynihan said, "is not to say, you, Johnny Brown, 11 years old...can go and climb Mount Hood, (but) to say, isn't it fun to climb a mountain; and there must be a mountain or even a hill somewhere in your neighborhood that you can try."

The production crews shoot 16mm synchronous sound during the "events" and, after each experience, the children are inter-

Fig. 4-3. One of the highlights of 12-year-old Matty Levine's visit to the capital of country music is meeting and performing with the famous dobro (a special type of steel guitar) player, Brother Oswald. Matty, a New Jersey resident, spends a week with country star Bobby Bare and his family as hosts for the half-hour "Call It Macaroni" special, "Nashville, Over the Rainbow." (Photo courtesy of Group W Productions).

viewed on audiotape. The crew usually spends a week shooting. The producers visit each location, selected a month in advance, and walk through every step of the adventure themselves, so that they will know what to expect and to make sure that the activities are within the capabilities of the children and that the whole activity is safe.

The series has produced good audiences for the Westinghouse stations and has been syndicated to help defray the rather high cost of production—approximately $33,000 per episode.

Moynihan reports that they have attempted to get feedback about the program and found that children in the audience perceived the series as was hoped—as an example of children doing things which they might be able to do in the same circumstances.

It's interesting to note that this example of quality programming for children has proven saleable. The Westinghouse executive admits that the group's ability to syndicate the program to other markets has been important in paying its cost.

"Call It Macaroni" has been honored with the Peabody, Ohio State and ACT (Action for Children's Television) awards (Fig. 4-3).

"Snipets"

The programmers at Kaiser Broadcasting also desired to develop improved programming for children. However, at the time, Kaiser was struggling to make its chain of UHF stations profitable and so budgetary limitations had to be considered.

Kaiser's Director of Children's Program Development, Frank A. Philpot, explained his strategy: "We decided that the best way to maximize our resources was to produce a series of short spots, each of which would stand alone. These spots would then be played within our popular children's entertainment programming. Each spot could be played many times over a long period...thus maximizing our program investment; and we felt sure that we could reach a much larger audience than with a weekly half-hour program. We thought of this as our 'sugar-coated-pill theory' of children's educational programming." (Fig. 4-4).

Philpot added: "We recruited three academic experts—a child psychologist and two experts in communication theory—to advise us during the initial development of the series.

"We produced 'Snipets' using both animation and live action and have focused on a variety of topics including: nutrition, bicycle

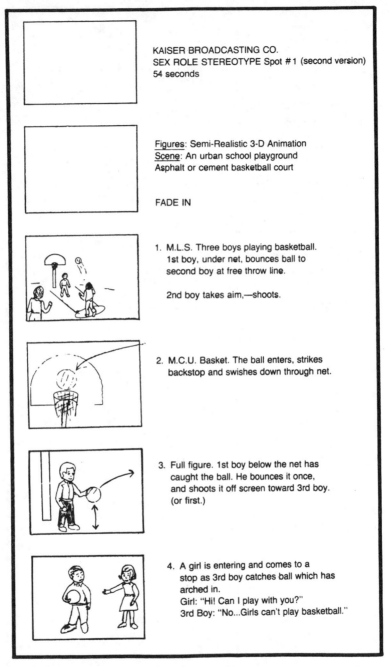

KAISER BROADCASTING CO.
SEX ROLE STEREOTYPE Spot #1 (second version)
54 seconds

Figures: Semi-Realistic 3-D Animation
Scene: An urban school playground
Asphalt or cement basketball court

FADE IN

1. M.L.S. Three boys playing basketball.
   1st boy, under net, bounces ball to
   second boy at free throw line.

   2nd boy takes aim,—shoots.

2. M.C.U. Basket. The ball enters, strikes
   backstop and swishes down through net.

3. Full figure. 1st boy below the net has
   caught the ball. He bounces it once,
   and shoots it off screen toward 3rd boy.
   (or first.)

4. A girl is entering and comes to a
   stop as 3rd boy catches ball which has
   arched in.
   Girl: "Hi! Can I play with you?"
   3rd Boy: "No...Girls can't play basketball."

Fig. 4-4. Storyboard for Kaiser Broadcasting Company "Snipet" feature (Courtesy Kaiser Broadcasting Company). (Continued on pages 88 and 89.)

5. CU Girl: "Why not?"
   Boy: (OC) "Just because....Everybody
   knows that."

6. Closer on both of them.

   Boy: (cont.) "Watch!....can you do this?"
   (he takes aim, makes a long, one-arm
   shot.)

7. M.S. Ball enters, arcs high through
   frame and swishes down through
   net without touching backstop
   or hoop.

8. S.A. scene 6. (Girl holds out hands for
   boy off screen to throw it to her.)

   Girl: "I can try."......(She catches
   ball which enters, takes aim and shoots
   the same way boy did.)

9. Sky or skyline.

   The ball arcs high into frame and
   down and out other side.

10. Close on the net, as in scene 2. Low
    angle.

    The ball arcs down swishing through net.

Fig. 4-4. (Continued from page 87 and continued on page 89.)

11. ¾ figure, girl.

    Girl: "See, all it takes is practice."

12. Full figure boy: (he already has the ball.)

    3rd boy: "Okay,---how about this one?" (he attempts a hook shot.)

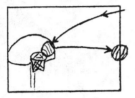

13. M.S. The net. Ball arcs down, strikes hoop, bounces out of frame.

14. Full figure girl. (The ball enters on a bounce, and she catches it.)

    Girl: "Now let me give it a try." (she duplicates his attempt.)

15. M.S. The Net.
Ball arcs down, hits backstop, then rim of hoop, bounces out of frame.

16. 2-shot. Boy and Girl:

    Girl: (disappointed) "Missed!"
    3rd boy: (smiling) "I guess we could both use some more practice--- come on. You can be on my team!"

    FADE OUT

THE END

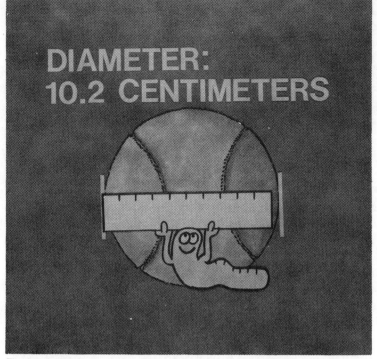

Fig. 4-5. An illustration from a Kaiser Broadcasting Company "Snipet" feature on the metric system. (Photo courtesy of Kaiser Broadcasting Co.)

safety, sex role stereotypes, art appreciation, childhood fears, and simply toys and games children can make for themselves." Other projects discussed included "Snipets" on attitudes toward handicapped persons, the elderly, the metric system and ethnic pride (Fig. 4-5).

Most stations find children's programming a difficult and challenging task. In general this type of programming seems to place heavy demands on facilities and often requires considerable production help to handle the selection and scheduling of guests. For these reasons, television stations tend to rely heavily on syndicated programs and features.

There are even organizations which provide prepackaged live children's formats. This is one reason we see "Romper Room" in market after market.

For the most part the program departments of most television stations have responsibility for children's programming. However, there are alert public affairs dierctors who include people interested in the problem of mass media and children among their interview guests. There are public affairs directors who get help from school systems and universities, and make their mark by developing solid children's informational programming. "CBS News" has made a major step in this direction with its brief Saturday-morning segments that explain that week's news to children.

It can be safely predicted that the outcry for quality children's programming will not die down for a long time. Stations can be expected to be called on to do more and better, both in their commercial and public affairs programming.

Chapter 5
Legal Requirements

This chapter will review a number of legal requirements of the Federal Communications Commission which are directly pertinent to public affairs programming. Our major concentration will be on the important and relatively new obligation of radio and television stations to "ascertain" their markets. Ascertainment is the systematic process of seeking out major problems, interests and needs affecting a community. Tied to this is a positive obligation to devise programs which deal with these problems, and then demonstrate to the FCC that all this has been done.

ASCERTAINMENT

Ascertainment is a requirement which must be documented each time a radio or television station files for renewal of its license. The obligation affects commercial and non-commercial stations, but, for the sake of our discussion, we will list only the rules affecting commercial stations.

Initially some broadcasters found requirements for systematic interviews of community leaders and periodic surveys of the general public a bit frightening. However, most broadcasters have gained sufficient experience since the process started in 1971 to treat the obligation calmly. Some, naturally, complain about the proliferation of paperwork, but many station executives admit they are making use of the information they gather from their ascertainment interviews.

What follows is a description of the various regulations contained in the January 1976 revision of the ascertainment rules.

Demographic Showing

The licensee must maintain, in a public file, a listing of the demographic characteristics of its city of license. These include:

1. Total population figures
2. Numbers and proportions of:
   a. males and females
   b. minorities
   c. youth (17 and under)
   d. the elderly (65 and older)

The Commission points out that the needed demographic data is contained in two U.S. Census Bureau publications, *County and City Data Book* and *General Population Characteristics*. Inclusion of information on areas outside the station's service area is optional.

The demographic area covered by the ascertainment regulations extends no more than 75 miles from the city of license, less, if the station's coverage area is less. Communities outside this 75-mile limit do not need to be ascertained.

Who Must Ascertain

The only commercial stations excluded from meeting all the requirements of the ascertainment program are those in communities of 10,000 population or less, which are located outside all Standard Metropolitan Statistical Areas. This exempts only a handful of television stations and about 1900 radio stations.

The SMSA requirement was inserted to prevent radio stations whose city of license happens to be a small, suburban community within a larger metropolitan area from exercising this exemption.

The exclusion does not mean that qualifying stations may omit filing ascertainment data at renewal time. It simplifies the data. The Commission requires that small market stations file an "Annual Problems-Programs List," demonstrating that the station is conversant with and reacts to the needs of the community. But the Commission does not require Community Leader Interviews, General

Public Surveys, a Community Leader Checklist or demographic data.

Everyone else must follow the ascertainment guidelines.

The major change instituted between 1971 and 1976 was the switch from ascertaining during the six months prior to filing for renewal to ascertaining, continuously, over the three-year license period. This had generally met with broadcaster approval, since there is plenty of other data to be compiled just prior to renewal time, without having to do a full series of interviews.

Community Leader Interviews

The Community Leader Interviews are the backbone of the FCC's ascertainment program. The Commission wants each station to select a representative cross-section of community leaders and have management representatives interview these leaders face-to-face in order to learn about the needs, problems and interests these leaders detect in the community.

The rules are not absolute. Not all interviews have to be done by management and not all interviews have to be face-to-face, but the majority do have to meet the requirements, which we will discuss subsequently.

The FCC, in an attempt to codify the process, has devised a list of 19 categories which it calls the Community Leader Checklist. It serves as a guide for stations in planning their interviews and as a checklist for the Commission in analyzing the station's ascertainment program.

The list:

1. Agricultural
2. Business
3. Charities
4. Civic, neighborhood and fraternal organizations
5. Consumer services
6. Culture
7. Education
8. Environment
9. Government (local, county, state and federal)
10. Labor
11. Military

12. Minority and ethic groups
13. Organizations of and for the elderly
14. Organizations of and for women
15. Organizations of and for the youth (including children and students)
16. Professions
17. Public safety, health and welfare
18. Recreation
19. Religion
20. Other

If a station feels there are some other major categories to be interviewed, it may list them. But, as in all things devised by the federal bureaucracy, stations are now in the position of having to either demonstrate they have conducted interviews in the 19 categories outlined, or provide a valid explanation why a category or categories were omitted.

So, for practical reasons, the first guideline becomes,—do interviews for each of the 19 categories. How many interviews? Well the FCC approached this problem by outlining a "gross quantitative sufficiency" standard for different size markets.

Table 5-1. Gross Quantitative Sufficiency

Population of City of License	Number of Consultations
10,001 to 25,000	60
25,001 to 50,000	100
50,001 to 200,000	140
200,001 to 500,000	180
Over 500,000	220

If your station meets the minimum outlined for your community of license (according to population), then the Commission will not challenge the ascertainment program on a quantitative basis.

The total minimum must be accomplished within the term of the license.

That takes care of the quantitative minimums, which most stations choose to exceed on the advice of their counsel. Then, there is the question of *qualitative* factors.

One way to flunk the qualitative test would be to omit a category and not provide a satisfactory explanation for the omission. The qualitative question could be raised if some of the more outspoken groups, such as women or minorities, were left out. Communications lawyers suggest that interviews of representatives of women's and minority groups be done *only* by management personnel, as a precaution in case of a challenge to a renewal application.

How do you do community leader interviews? The interviews should be conducted throughout the three-year term of the license, and the Commission requires that summaries of the interviews be put into a public file within 30 to 45 days after they are completed.

A form should be prepared for each interview indicating the following:

The name and address of the community leader.

The institution or element of the community represented.

The date, time and place of the interview.

Problems, needs or interests discussed during the interview (unless the leader requests that the responses be kept confidential).

The name of the licensee representative conducting the interview.

When a non-manager conducts the interview, the name of the principal or management level employee who reviewed the complete interview record.

All forms must be on file for the period prior to the date on which the licensee files for renewal with the FCC.

It used to be that 100 percent of the interviews had to be conducted by management level employees. But the latest regulations permit up to 50 percent of the interviews to be conducted by non-management level employees, providing their worksheets are reviewed and signed by a member of management.

This change is especially important for stations with small staffs, because other staff members may conduct the interviews, as long as their work is reviewed. As an example, the host of a public affairs program might take a little time before or after the program and do an ascertainment interview. After the fact sheet has been prepared, the program manager would review and sign it.

There is a strong feeling among some advisors that it is unwise to take full advantage of the 50 percent rule, and that as near to 100 percent of the interviews as possible should be done by management level employees. This could include, for example, the general manager, sales manager, program manager, chief engineer, production director, public affairs director, community affairs director, editorial director, operations manager, promotion manager and, depending on the station's view of the idea, the news director.

Many stations divide up the monthly quota and give a certain number of interviews to each management-level individual. Later someone reviews and collates the paperwork and makes a summary which is circulated to management-level employees, so that all the decision-makers will be aware of the community issues which have been listed by community leaders. It is then up to the management to see that the station's programming, especially in the public affairs' area, addresses itself to those major areas of concern.

As we mentioned earlier, the ascertainment interviews should be predominantly face-to-face interviews, either in the leader's office or at the station. They may develop out of another meeting, or be scheduled independently, but the ascertainment part of the interview should be structured separately from other business discussed, and should include the data needed to complete an ascertainment form.

Many stations do what is called "informal ascertainment" which is simply keeping a diary of informal contacts—usually telephone conversations—in addition to meeting the formal ascertainment requirements.

The FCC, in its own publication on the ascertainment program, suggests that, in some cases where community leaders remain stable over a number of years in a particular category, the station might revisit them for follow-up interviews, which are counted as new and separate ascertainments.

Conversely, the Commission also points out that the station should make "reasonable and good faith" efforts to consult with many leaders and not return to the same people just because they are cooperative or convenient.

While face-to-face interviews are regarded as the most important type of interview, the FCC permits limited use of the telephone. Most station lawyers discourage taking this option.

Normally, an on-the-air appearance by a community leader cannot be used as an ascertainment item. (However, this does show some degree of discharge of your obligation to meet and discuss community needs.)

The Commission makes an exception when, during the course of the program, the leader, "reveals a community problem, need or interest which results in the consideration of a future program concerning that problem, need or interest." Most stations formalize this for ascertainment purposes by simply sitting down with the guest before or after the program to do an ascertainment interview.

Many stations keep careful tabs on guests coming into the studios, so that ascertainment interviews can be done with the appropriate people while they are in the building. One major New York City station takes this approach to the extent of having a clerk assigned to keep track of guests and inform the appropriate executives.

It's obviously more effective to take a few minutes from the in-station work day to do an ascertainment, rather than have to travel to do the interview.

The Commission does permit group interviews, providing all the stations and all the leaders participating get an ample opportunity for interchange. The FCC also feels that there should be something in common among the group of interviewees. Some radio stations in medium and large markets use this technique to cut down on the number of different interviews the leaders have to participate in, often repeating their responses.

Another possibility is to structure a community leader luncheon to meet the needs of the ascertainment program. There may even be occasions during news interviews when an ascertainment form could be completed, although many stations prefer not to involve reporters in the ascertainment process.

The Community Leader Checklist. The FCC does NOT require a licensee to send in the individual ascertainment interview forms. These must simply be kept in a public file at the station.

The list contains the 19 categories mentioned earlier, tabulates the number of leaders interviewed in each category, and provides any explanations needed if no leaders were interviewed in a category. The suggested form (which follows, plus a sample Leader Contact Form) also asks for a tabulation of how many of the leaders interviewed were:

Institution/Element	Number	Not Applicable (Explain briefly)
1. Agriculture		
2. Business		
3. Charities		
4. Civic, Neighborhood and Fraternal Organizations		
5. Consumer Services		
6. Culture		
7. Education		
8. Environment		
9. Government (local, county, state & federal)		
10. Labor		
11. Military		
12. Minority and ethnic groups		
13. Organizations of and for the Elderly		
14. Organizations of and for Women		
15. Organizations of and for Youth (including children) and Students		
16. Professions		
17. Public Safety, Health and Welfare		
18. Recreation		
19. Religion		
20. Other		
While the following are not regarded as separate community elements for purposes of this survey, indicate the number of leaders interviewed in all elements above who are:		
(a) Blacks		
(b) Hispanic, Spanish speaking or Spanish-surnamed Americans		
(c) American Indians		
(d) Orientals		
(e) Women		

Fig. 5-1. Sample Ascertainment Forms (Courtesy Federal Communications Commission).

Blacks

Hispanic, Spanish-speaking or Spanish-surnamed Americans

American Indians

Oriental

Women

It is entirely possible that a leader may qualify for tabulation on more than one list.

Samples of a Community Leader Annual Checklist and a Leader Contact Form are shown in Figs. 5-1 and 5-2.

General Public Survey

Up to this point we have talked about a process of consulting community leaders. The FCC also requires that a station conduct a General Public Survey for its renewal application.

100

Date: ____________

Name and address of person contacted: ____________

____

____

Organization(s) or group(s) represented by person contacted: ____________

____

Date, time and place of contact: ____________

____

Method of contact: ____________

____

Problems, needs and interests identified by person contacted: ____________

____

____

____

____

____

____

Name of interviewer: ____________

Reviewed by ____________ Position ____________

Date ____________

Fig. 5-2. Suggested Leader Contact Form (Courtesy Federal Communications Commission).

The FCC does not specify exactly how to do the survey, except to say that it should achieve "randomness" and that documentation relating to the methodology must be on file. Two suggestions mentioned in Commission documents include random selection using the telephone book and geographically distributed, man-on-the-street or questionnaire interviews. The Commission requires that an indication of the number of interviews and a full description of technique used to achieve a "roughly random sample" be on file.

The survey has the same purpose as the leader interviews—to discover problems, needs and interests among a random sampling of members of the general public. It is not a survey of programming preferences.

The Commission does not define randomness, hence it does not set standards for the number of interviews. The FCC does say that the survey need only be done in the city of license. Guidance on the question of randomness can be obtained by checking standard textbooks on statistics.

Fortunately for many station licensees, the Commission permits the use of an outside survey organization or consultant to design and or conduct the public survey. The Commission DOES NOT permit anyone outside the licensee organization to conduct leader interviews.

The survey can be done anytime during the license term, but must be on file at renewal filing time, or within 30 to 45 days after the survey is completed. This means that you should plan on having the survey materials tabulated promptly.

The Commission states that the documentation required after the survey shall consist of: "A narrative statement concerning the method used to conduct the general public survey, the number of people consulted, and the ascertain results of the survey." (FCC, Ascertainment of Community Problems by Broadcast Applicants—Primer; 1976 p., 1382.)

This information is put on file, and for renewal, the licensee simply certifies that the required information is held in station files.

Programming in Response to the Interviews and Survey

The second part of the ascertainment program is to indicate to the FCC that the station has aired programming, which has been responsive to the problems, needs and interests discovered in the leader and public interviews.

The Commission requires that each year the licensee place in its public file a list of what it considers to be the significant problems in the community, and a list of some of the programs it aired to respond to these problems.

Many stations, particularly radio stations, have rather narrowly defined target audiences and narrowly defined programming. The

Commission makes the blanket statement that "all members of the public are entitled to some service from each station," but then leaves it to the station licensee's "good faith judgment" to take into consideration the station's format and audience, as well as the programming of other stations in the market. (FCC, Ascertainment of Community Problems by Broadcast Applicants—Primer; 1976.)

The Commission doesn't specify just what sort of programming would be appropriate to respond to community problems, but it does strongly suggest that news coverage and public service announcements alone do not fulfill the perceived need, largely due to their brevity.

The Commission does say that the type of programming can be tailored to a station's format but does suggest it be in sufficient depth to adequately discuss the problem. Ironically, the Commission does not regard an all-news format as automatically discharging this obligation, unless there is special programming within the format to deal with the ascertained problems.

Some of the elements which may be counted include: programs, news and public service announcements, editorial, ordinary and special news inserts, and program vignettes. What the Commission is saying is that the programming must devote sufficient time to a problem to permit adequate treatment of the topic. The exact method or methods used are up to the licensee.

On the matter of documentation: The Commission requires the licensee to place in its public inspection file—on each anniversary date of the filing of the station's license renewal application—a list of no more than ten significant problems, needs and interests ascertained during the 12 preceding months. The licensee must then indicate "typical and illustrative" programs broadcast in response to these ten problems, needs or interests. The specific information which must be included is:

The title of the program or program series.
It's source.
It's type.
A brief description of the program.
Broadcast time and duration.

The FCC says this list does not include public service announcements or news inserts of breaking events.

The license renewal will include an "Annual Problems—Program List" for each of the three years of the license term.

One footnote—if a renewal applicant has conducted an ascertainment survey within the 12 months before renewal for some other purpose, the survey need not be done again, as long as it meets the general requirements for a survey.

ASCERTAINMENT AS SEEN BY COMMERCIAL STATIONS

We solicited comments from a number of broadcast station executives.

Larry Williams is general manager of WBLX radio in Mobile, Alabama. Williams believes in doing ascertainment interviews on a daily basis. Each week he, the sales manager, program director and news director have a quota of five interviews which must be completed. Williams plans to do at least two of these interviews himself.

Every Tuesday the ascertainment group meets and Williams approves a schedule of target interviews.

He attempts to set up an interview with a specific individual from the target list. Failing this, Williams immediately selects an alternate and makes certain that his quota is filled. Williams also makes it a policy to revisit interviewees after a few months to see if their ideas on major issues facing the community have changed, or if they have adjusted their priorities.

The station's community affairs director is responsible for keeping the general manager informed about guests being interviewed at the WBLX studios. When possible, these guests are ascertained BEFORE they are interviewed. This technique allows for a good warm up of the guest and allows for interview guests who want to leave promptly after the interview program is completed.

At WSBK television in Boston, the management group consists of three key persons: the general manager, the station manager and the program manager. They try to do 20 or 30 interviews a month, half of which are done right in the building with people who have come to appear on programs.

Jim Hart, who was general manager of WXII-TV in Winston-Salem, North Carolina, talked about the revised ascertainment program. He said: "I think continuing ascertainment makes a lot more sense than the jam-packed six months right before your licensee renewal....And the guidelines seem to be flexible enough. I don't think they are unreasonable in the light of the population that we serve. If anything, we'll far exceed the number that they (FCC) might loosely recommend as a minimum for a market this size or cities of the size that we serve."

Hart added: "There are some groups that are listed among the...groups to be ascertained that are very difficult to get representatives from...it is very time consuming." He cited an example: "Labor, for instance, they are very suspicious of the media, when they do make appointments, they won't show up when we go to them, they won't come here, period...oftentimes, they won't be there, they won't return phone calls."

Hart continued: "Usually members of a minority are more than willing, in fact anxious, to speak up and so are women's groups. The problem we have is making sure that these people represent a viable part of whatever group we're going after. We only want to interview these people in so far as they're part of a specific group of their own."

WXII has a system set up to ascertain guests on the station's weekday midmorning interview program. The target is to complete 25 to 30 ascertainments a month. One concern of Hart's was making sure that his staff gets out to ascertain in the many small communities which dot the rural North Carolina and Virginia areas served by his station.

Hart said his station tries to program as it goes along to meet the problems brought out in the ascertainment process.

At WFSB-TV in Hartford, Connecticut, Vice President for Public Affairs Dick Ahles said: "The main source of ideas has to be the ascertainment process....We know that we are obliged to do programs that respond... When I go out and ascertain...I'm pretty sure I'll come back with an idea for at least one segment on a magazine show out of it. That's fine, and that makes it worthwhile."

WFSB's ascertainment program is directed by a man who was the station's news director for many years and is now an advisor to the general manager. Each month the information from all of the station's ascertainment interviews is compiled and summarized. This summary is circulated in a memo defining problems for consideration by the station's top executives.

WFSB has a larger management structure, so it is possible to assign four or six interviews a month to the 15 to 20 responsible station employees.

Ahles had an interesting observation about the information which comes out of ascertainment interviews: "We find, very frankly, that what we ascertain in Hartford (the city of license) isn't all that different than what we ascertain in New Haven and Springfield, the other large cities in the market. The smaller towns are different, we almost know what we're going to get when we go out to ascertain anybody—we've been doing it so long."

The ascertainment lists are compiled through the knowledge of station executives, plus the use of lists provided by outside organizations such as chambers of commerce, civic groups and governmental units.

Charles Sanford is vice-president and general manager of WGAN-AM-FM-TV in Portland Maine. He recounted an experience in a nearby city in his coverage area. "I was up in Lewiston, talking with the mayor, police chief, superintendent of schools, those people—about the problems of the community, and I found it quite difficult to really extract from them what really were the problems of the community."

He said the mayor was concerned primarily about internal political problems which blocked certain programs.

Another example cited by Sanford. FBI statistics indicated a rapid growth in certain categories of crime, but he found it difficult to get any acknowledgement from police chiefs that they were having problems.

Sanford makes it a policy to sit down with his radio and television news directors, following a series of ascertainment interviews, and discuss the issues brought out.

THE PUBLIC SURVEY—AN EXAMPLE

To people not acquainted with survey techniques, the idea of doing or having a survey done can be a bit frightening.

In an attempt to dispell some of those fears, and yet avoid a long and technical discourse on survey techniques, we are reproducing a portion of a survey summary prepared in January 1976 by the Communications Research Center of the College of Journalism and

Communications at the University of Florida for educational station WUFT-TV. The survey excerpts are reproduced here with the College's permission. The survey deals with one aspect not required by the FCC because WUFT wanted to make some determinations about program preferences as part of its survey. However, the discussion of methodology and cost-saving techniques will be instructive. Note, also, that the geographic range of the WUFT survey is greater than that required by the FCC. The Commission requires only that the survey be conducted within the city of license.

The example which follows should suggest to commercial broadcasters that, in addition to utilizing commercial survey firms, they have the alternative of having the survey done by the faculty of a nearby college or university, or by their own staff, with faculty members acting as consultants.

Selection of the Sample. First, it was necessary to have a defined population, that is, the group about which we wished to make inferences. The population was defined as all the residents of the viewing area, 18 years of age or older (excluding those in institutions such as prisons, hospitals, etc.). According to most current estimates, this group contains 461,245 persons in 122,395 households.

Table 5-2. County-By-County Breakdown of Sample Size.

County	Population	Sample Size
Alachua	120,128	104
Baker	10,886	10
Bradford	15,254	13
Citrus	30,253	26
Clay	41,436	36
Columbia	27,093	22
Dixie	5,885	10
Gilchrist	4,095	10
Hamilton	4,023	10
Lafayette	3,072	7
Levy	13,944	12
Marion	83,327	74
Putnam	40,507	35
St. Johns	35,992	32
Suwannee	16,561	18
Union	8,789	10
TOTAL	461,245	429

Stratified random sampling, a form of probability sampling, was used for choosing respondents. This technique insures that each element (in this case, a person) has a chance of selection. It also provides a known margin of error for inferences about the entire population. When using stratified random sampling, the population is divided into distinct groups (strata) and a random sample is taken from each group. In this case each stratum represented one county.

Using a statistical formula, the sample size for the total viewing area was determined to be 429 with a maximum bound on error of .05. In other words, all percentages reported would be accurate to within at least five percentage points 95 percent of the time. The total sample size of 429 was then broken down into 16 strata sample sizes in proportion to the population of each county. Table 5-2 contains a county-by-county breakdown of the sample size.

Economic and manpower considerations entered into decisions concerning the method of data collection. Three methods were considered: the mail survey, the telephone interview, or the personal (face-to-face) interview. The mail survey was deemed unacceptable for this study, due to its built-in factor of self-selection among respondents and a probable low response rate. The personal interview requires a great deal of time and expense, due to the travel involved. Not only must the cost of transportation be considered, but since the process is a slow one, more interviewers are required to complete the interviews than with other methods. Much of the viewing area is rural, which would make this type of data collection technique complicated for interviewers and costly for the station.

The telephone interview, on the other hand, makes it possible to collect the necessary information while keeping limitations to a minimum. The possibility of respondent self-selection is lessened, since most people find it more difficult to refuse an interviewer verbally than to throw away a mail questionnaire. The telephone interview is also more efficient in terms of cost and travel time, since all interviews in an area are conducted from one central location. Based on these considerations, the telephone survey was chosen as the most effective method for gathering the data.

The next step in the research design was the acquisition of a frame, or listing of all the elements of households in the population. The most obvious choice when using telephones to conduct the survey is the telephone book. Use of phone directories limits the definition of the population to those persons who have telephones and whose phone numbers are listed, but this was not considered a serious shortcoming for the WUFT study.

Having determined both the sample size and the frame, the next step was to select survey respondents. First, the sample size for each county was broken down into several smaller sample sizes for each city and its surrounding area, in proportion to the population. Then, going to the section of the phone book for that city, a table of random numbers was used to select survey respondents. In addition, 30 percent more were chosen in order to have a list of alternates to be called in the event of non-respondents.

Data Collection. For some time work had been underway on the instrument of data collection—the questionnaire. An earlier study, similar to the present one but confined to Gainesville, provided the foundation. Program producers and directors were asked to suggest any additional questions which would provide them with useful information. After several drafts, pretesting, and extensive discussion, the final form of the questionnaire was developed.

Two training sessions were held for the interviewers. In the first they received a notebook containing a questionnaire and information on the station, its history and programming. The station program manager spoke to them briefly and answered questions. They were instructed to familiarize themselves with the questionnaire and the phone log which they would keep when interviewing. At the second training session, interviewers conducted five "practice" interviews on a selected sample of Gainesville residents.

Interviewers were told to ask to speak to the head of the household. If the household head was not available, the interviewer asked to speak to a male or female member of the household, 18 years of age or older. This was an attempt to maintain some consistency among respondents, and yet eliminate as much bias as possible.

Non-respondents were encountered for a variety of reasons: a disconnected phone, no answer, or refusal to answer the questions.

Table 5-3. Comparison of Population* and Sample by Sex.

Sex	Population	Sample
Male	49%	44%
Female	51	56

*Figures from U.S. Census Bureau (1970).

Table 5-4. Comparison of Population* and Sample by Race.

Race	Population	Sample
White	81%	89%
Non-White	19	11

*Figures from U.S. Census Bureau (1970).

In the case of refusals, interviewers were instructed to attempt to encourage answers, but not to engage in argument. When interviewers encountered any type of non-respondent, they went to the alternate list for the name of another respondent. During the evening interviewers called back any "no answers," which they encountered earlier in the evening, in an attempt to include the respondent in the survey.

In an attempt to establish credibility and a sense of legitimacy with the respondents, a short letter of introduction was sent before interviewing began. The letter, with data and approximate time of the interviewer's call typed in, was sent to each respondent. Since the only addresses available were those published in the phone books, about 16 percent of these letters could not be delivered.

All interviewing was conducted Sunday through Thursday, during the month of April, by a group of 10 male and female interviewers. Interviewing began promptly at 7 p.m. in order to have the best opportunity of catching the head of the household, probably a wage earner, at home. No call was made after 10 p.m.

Analysis. When the interviewing was completed, coding of the questionnaires for computer analysis began. The information from each questionnaire was punched in coded form onto three computer cards. Using the Statistical Package for the Social Sciences (SPSS) developed by Normal H. Nie *et al.* at the University of Chicago, raw figures, percentages, and tables were obtained.

In addition, comparison was made of the characteristics of survey respondents with those of the residents of the viewing area.

Table 5-5. Comparison of Population* and Sample by Age.

Age	Population	Sample
18-24	21%	13%
25-34	18	20
35-49	23	26
50-64	22	22
65 and over	16	19

*Figures from U.S. Census Bureau (1970).

110

It showed that the sample did provide a representative cross-section of the population. The proportions of men and women, whites and non-whites, and various age groups were very similar between the group of respondents and the population of the sixteen counties (see Tables 5-3, 5-4, 5-5).

GENERAL PUBLIC QUESTIONNAIRE

ID No.

Hello, My name is _____and I'm conducting a survey for the Communication Research Center at the Unversity of Florida. We are interested in your opinions about TV viewing.

Your household has been drawn in a random sample, and I need to ask a member of your household a few questions. It will take only a few minutes and all answers will be confidential.

Could I please speak to the head of the household?
(IF NONE AVAILABLE THEN—Could I speak to a male or female member of the household who is 18 years of age or older?)

(IF A NEW PERSON COMES TO THE PHONE, REPEAT THE FIRST TWO PARAGRAPHS BEFORE PROCEEDING.)

First, we are interested in your opinions about your community.

DO NOT PAUSE

1. How long have you lived in the _____area?

   _____

2. During this time, what have you found that you like best about the community in general?

   _____

   _____

3. What problems in the community are of the most concern to you?

   _____   _____

   _____   _____

   Probe: Are there any others?

4. In talking to others several common community problems have been mentioned. In the community, do you feel that_____is/are a problem?

CIRCLE RESPONSE	Problem	Not a Problem	Not Sure
streets & roads	1	2	3
law enforcement	1	2	3
traffic	1	2	3
utility rates	1	2	3
schools	1	2	3
jobs	1	2	3

DO NOT ASK ABOUT PROBLEMS WHICH RESPONDENT MENTIONED IN QUESTION THREE ABOVE.

5. Which one of these stands out in your mind as being most important? _____

_____

6. What do you think the_____community needs—such as new services or facilities?

_____

_____

_____

Probe: Are there any others?

IF ONLY ONE NAMED, GO TO 8

7. Which of these needs do you feel is the most urgent?

_____

8. How long have you lived in Florida?

_____

9. During this time, what problems in Florida have concerned you most?

_____

_____

Probe: Are there any others?

IF ONLY ONE NAMED, GO TO 11

10. Which of these appears to you to most pressing?

_____

11. On the national level, what problems in this country are of the most concern to you?

_____

_____

_____

Probe: Are there any others?

IF ONLY ONE NAMED, SKIP 12

12. Which of these do you think is the most critical?

_____

(Succeeding portions of this form are omitted because they deal only with programs.)

To help us with program planning, we need to know a little about your background and interests.

63. What is your occupation?

_____ NOTE: GET **SPECIFIC** JOB

65. What was the last grade of school or year of college that you attended?

_____ NOTE: IF TRADE SCHOOL GET LAST
YEAR OF HIGH SCHOOL

66. What is your age?

_____

67. Within a range, I'd like to know your family income for the last year. Was it......
    1 ( ) under $3,000
    2 ( ) between $3,000 and $6,000
    3 ( ) between $6,000 and $10,000
    4 ( ) between $10,000 and $15,000
    5 ( ) between $15,000 and $20,000
    6 ( ) over $20,000

68. Whether or not you attend services regularly—what is your religious preference?

_____

69. Again, to help us in programming, what is your race?

_____

THAT CONCLUDES THE INTERVIEW. THANK YOU VERY MUCH FOR YOUR TIME AND COOPERATION.

70. RECORD, DO NOT ASK

    Sex   1   ( ) Male   2   ( ) Female

RESPONDENT "THANK YOU" POSTCARD

Thank you very much for your time and cooperation with our research project. All information received from study respondents such as yourself will greatly aid us in planning our television programming to better serve you.

Sincerely,

Project Director

INITIAL RESPONDENT CONTACT LETTER

In an attempt to insure that TV programming keeps pace with the special needs, problems and interests of the public, the Communication Research Center is conducting a survey in your area to determine just what the problems, needs and interests of people in your community are.

Your household has been drawn in a random sample and will represent 1,000 homes. An interviewer will call you.

Your cooperation is very important to the success of this study. All information which you give us will be strictly confidential and used only to help us with TV programming decisions.

If you have any questions about this study, please call the Communication Research Center (904-000-000).

Thank you for your help.

Sincerely,

Project Director

AGREEMENTS BETWEEN LICENSEES AND THE PUBLIC

There has been an increasing trend in the broadcast industry for community groups to establish contractual relationships with broadcasters, concerning such areas as minority-oriented programming and employment of women and minorities.

The FCC has taken cognizance of these agreements, and has set forth certain policies regarding such agreements.

The Commission, first of all, reminds licensees that they alone bear the ultimate responsibility for the "planning, execution and supervision of programming and station operation." (Agreements

Between Broadcast Licensees and the Public; Docket 20495; FCC 75–1359, Dec. 10, 1975.) This means that any agreement must NOT abdicate control of programming or facilities to a non-license group.

The FCC leaves the decision up to the licensee as to whether negotiations will be carried on with any community group. The Commission has stated that it sees no reason to penalize a licensee for failing to meet with a particular group.

The Commission goes even further by telling licensees they should reject proposals by any group which the licensee feels does not represent the public interest.

The Commission requires that if a contract is drawn up with a community group, a copy of the contract must be placed in the station's public file. The FCC does NOT require that a copy of the agreement be forwarded to the Commission unless the licensee so desires. If the licensee does want to forward the document to the FCC, the Commission suggests that the contract be handled as an amendment to the most recent renewal application or other pertinent application.

The parties to this sort of agreement can request that a copy of the agreement be placed in the station's public file at the FCC. The Commission says it does not expect this to be generally done, except in cases where the agreement is part of an application or is in response to a complaint.

The FCC points out that even though an agreement may be reached regarding, say, programming or employment practices, it cannot be immutable if the public interest demands that the basic premises in the agreements be altered. Among other things, the station cannot surrender the flexibility it needs to meet its obligation to serve the public interest, convenience and necessity.

The FCC says it will accept two review and enforcement responsibilities:

a. It will review an agreement to determine if it is contrary to statutes, rules or policies, if asked.

b. It will treat, as a representation to the Commission, any substantive agreement terms incorporated in an application. These terms will be considered promises of future performance.

The agreements must be written, not oral.

PUBLIC NOTICE

The FCC requires radio and television stations to make announcements at regular intervals, which inform the public of the licensee's obligations to the public and of how they can communicate their comments to the station.

The announcements must be made on the first and 16th days of the month, except "during the period beginning on the first day of the sixth full calendar month prior to expiration, and ending the last day of the next to last full calendar month prior to expiration, during which the renewal application notices in (FCC Section) 1.580(d)...shall be broadcast." (FCC Rules 73.1202.)

There are specific times during which the announcement must be made:

For commercial television stations: Between 6 p.m. and 11 p.m. (5 p.m. and 10 p.m. Central and Mountain time), for the announcement on the first day of the month. For the announcement of the 16th day, a rotating pattern is used—you rotate the following four-hour time periods, 6 a.m. to 10 a.m.; 10 a.m. to 2 p.m.; 2 p.m. to 6 p.m. The rotation begins with 6 a.m. to 10 a.m.

For commercial radio stations: The announcement on the first day of the calendar month is to be broadcast, either between 7 a.m. and 9 a.m., or between 4 p.m. and 6 p.m.

The announcement broadcast on the 16th day of the month is to be broadcast in rotating order as follows: 9 a.m. to 1 p.m.; 1 p.m. to 4 p.m.; 6 p.m. to 10 p.m. Since many stations operate on limited hours, there is the following exception: "For stations which neither operate between 7 a.m. and 9 a.m. nor between 4 p.m. and 6 p.m., the announcement broadcast on the first day of each calendar month shall be broadcast during the first two hours of broadcast operation and the announcement broadcast on the sixteenth day of each month shall be broadcast during every other four-hour time period during the broadcast day in rotating order, beginning with the third to sixth hours of broadcast operation." (FCC Rules 73,1202.)

If an emergency arises which prevents broadcast on the days specified, the notices should be broadcast on the next day following the emergency at the same designated times.

Television stations must show video, with the address to which the public may write, at the same time as the announcer is reading the address.

Here is the FCC's sample announcement for radio:

"On (date of last renewal grant (station's call letters) was granted a license by the Federal Communications Commission to serve the public interest as a public trustee until (date of license expiration). We are obligated to make a continuing, diligent effort to determine the significant problems and needs of our service area and to provide programming to help meet those problems and needs.

"We invite listeners to send specific suggestions or comments concerning our station's operation and programming efforts to (name and mailing address). Unless otherwise requested, all letters received will be available for public inspection during regular business hours."

The announcement for television might read as follows:

"On (date of last renewal grant) (Station's call letters) was granted a license by the Federal Communications Commission to serve the public interest as a public trustee until (date of license expiration). Each (anniversary date of deadline for filing renewal application) we place in our public inspection file a list of what we consider to have been some of the significant problems and needs of our service area during the preceding twelve months and some of our programming to help meet those problems and needs.

"We invite viewers to send specific suggestions or comments concerning our station operation and programming efforts to (name and mailing address). Unless otherwise requested, all letters received will be available for public inspection during regular business hours." (FCC Rules 73.1202.)

The Commission requires that all written comments and suggestions be kept in a file at the station which is available for inspection by the public. If the correspondent requests that the letter not be put in the public file, or in the judgment of the licensee the letter ought not be in a public file (perhaps it contains obscene or defamatory statements), it may be excluded from the public file. Letters must be retained for three years from date received.

THE PROGRAM LOG

All broadcast stations are required to keep minute-by-minute lists of the material they have broadcast. This list is referred to as the "log."

One requirement is that the program be identified by name or title. Broadcast stations, especially in radio, frequently identify short programs within longer programs separately, so that they may be counted in any analysis done to demonstrate the station's adherence to its public affairs obligations.

The FCC has developed its own list of program type definitions. Sometimes a program falls in more than one category.

The categories which are important to public affairs executives are:

Agricultural programs (symbol A)—they contain information of interest to or specifically addressed to the agricultural population, including market reports, farming and other information.

News programs (symbol N) which, according to the FCC, include: "reports dealing with current local, national, and international events, including weather and stock market reports; and when an integral part of a news program, commentary, analysis, and sports news."

Public Affairs Programs (PA)—in the language of the FCC include: "....talks, commentaries, discussions, speeches, editorials, political programs, documentaries, forums, panels, roundtables, and similar programs primarily concerning local, national, and international public affairs."

Religious programs (symbol R) which can include religious news, sermons, music, drama and other types of religious programs.

Instructional programs (symbol I) which are defined by the FCC as: "programs involving the discussion of, or primarily designed to further an appreciation or understanding of, literature, music, fine arts, history, geography, and the natural and social sciences; and programs devoted to occupational and vocational instruction, instruction with respect to hobbies, and similar programs intended primarily to instruct.

Editorials (symbol EDIT)

Political programs (symbol POL), which the FCC says, include: "those which present candidates for public office or which give expressions (other than in station editorials) to views on such candidates or on issues subject to public ballot."

Educational Institutions (ED)

The Federal Communications Commission also has a formal definition of a public service announcement. It is:

A public service announcement is an announcement for which no charge is made and which promotes programs, activities, or services of Federal, State, or local governments (e.g., recruiting, sales of bonds, etc.) or the programs, activities or services of nonprofit organizations (e.g., UGF, Red Cross Blood Donations, etc.) and other announcements regarded as serving community interests, excluding time signals, routine weather announcements and promotional announcements.

RENEWAL FORMS

The FCC renewal form requires the applicant station to analyze program logs from a composite week—a week arbitrarily derived by the FCC by selecting a single day and date from each of seven months.

The information sought asks that the broadcaster break out statistics for news, public affairs, all other program exclusive of entertainment and sports, and statistics listing numbers of public service announcements.

The comparison chart is based on three sets of figures: the time previously proposed, the composite week performance and the minimum proposed in terms of minutes of total time and percent of total time.

The renewal document asks for a listing of the programs included in the public affairs and "all other" categories. The listing must include title, source, type, a brief description, time broadcast and duration of each program.

We are not attempting to delve deeply into the renewal process, which is something which must be done with skilled legal advice. Our point is to warn you of some of the information you will need to be able to locate.

Letters received by television stations must be separated into "programming" and "non-programming" categories. If the viewer covers more than one category, the letter is to be filed in the dominant category.

THE NATIONAL ASSOCIATION OF BROADCASTERS CODES

The NAB Radio Code

What follows are some pertinent sections of The Radio Code of the National Association of Broadcasters (Twentieth Edition, June 1976). The code is a voluntary pledge which has been signed by many of the nation's radio stations.

PROGRAM STANDARDS

A. News

Radio is unique in its capacity to reach the largest number of people first with reports on current events. This competitive advantage bespeaks caution—being first is not as important as being accurate. The Radio Code standards relating to the treatment of news and public events are, because of constitutional considerations, intended to be exhortatory. The standards set forth hereunder encourage high standards of professionalism in broadcast journalism. They are not to be interpreted as turning over to others the broadcaster's responsibility as to judgments necessary to news and public events programming.

4. *Editorializing.* Broadcasts in which stations express their own opinions about issues of general public interest should be clearly identified as editorials.

5. *Coverage of News and Public Events.* In the coverage of news and public events broadcasters should exercise their judgments consonant with the accepted standards of ethical journalism and should provide accurate, informed and adequate coverage.

6. *Placement of Advertising.* Broadcasters should exercise particular discrimination in the acceptance, placement and presenta-

tion of advertising in news program so that such advertising is clearly distinguishable from the news content.

B. Controversial Public Issues

1. Radio provides a valuable forum for the expression of responsible views on public issues of a controversial nature. Controversial public issues of importance to fellow citizens should give fair representation to opposing sides of issues.

2. Requests by individuals, groups or organizations for time to discuss their views on controversial public issues should be considered on the basis of their individual merits, and in the light of the contributions which the use requested would make to the public interest.

3. Discussion of controversial public issues should not be presented in a manner which would create the impression that the program is other than one dealing with a public issue.

C. Community Responsibility

1. Broadcasters and their staffs occupy a position of responsibility in the community and should conscientiously endeavor to be acquainted with its needs and characteristics to best serve the welfare of its citizens.

2. Requests for time for the placement of public service announcements or programs should be carefully reviewed with respect to the character and reputation of the group, campaign or organization involved, the public interest content of the message, and the manner of its presentation.

D. Political Broadcasts

1. Political broadcasts, or the dramatization of political issues designed to influence voters, shall be properly identified as such.

2. Political broadcasts should not be presented in a manner which would mislead listeners to believe that they are of any other character.
(Reference: Communications Act of 1934, as amended, Secs. 315 and 317, and FCC Rules and Regulations, Secs. 3.654, 3.657, 3.663, as discussed in NAB's "Political Broadcast Catechism & The Fairness Doctrine.")

3. Because of the unique character of political broadcasts and the necessity to retain broad freedoms of policy void of restrictive interference, it is incumbent upon all political candidates and all political parties to observe the canons of good taste and political ethics, keeping in mind the intimacy of broadcasting in the American home.

E. Advancement of Education and Culture

1. Because radio is an integral part of American life, there is inherent in radio broadcasting a continuing opportunity to enrich the experience of living through the advancement of education and culture.

2. Radio broadcasters, in augmenting the educational and cultural influences of the home, schools, religious institutions and institutions of higher education and other entities should:

(a) be thoroughly conversant with the educational and cultural needs and aspirtions of the community served;

(b) develop programming consonant with the stations particular target audience.

F. Religion and Religious Programming

1. Religious programming shall be presented by responsible individuals, groups or organizations.

2. Radio broadcasting reaches audiences of all creeds simultaneously. Therefore, both the advocates of broad or ecumenical religious precepts, and the exponents of specific doctrines, are urged to present their positions in a manner conducive to listener enlightenment on the role of religion in society.

G. Responsibility Toward Children

Broadcasters have a special responsibility to children. Programming which might reasonably be expected to hold the attention of children should be presented with due regard for its effect on children.

1. Programming should be based upon sound social concepts and should include positive sets of values which will allow children to become responsible adults, capable of coping with the challenges of maturity.

2. Programming should convey a reasonable range of the realities which exist in the world to help children make the transition to adulthood.

3. Programming should contribute to the healthy development of personality and character.

4. Programming should afford opportunities for cultural growth as well as for wholesome entertainment.

5. Programming should be consistent with integrity of realistic production, but should avoid material of extreme nature which might create undesirable emotional reaction in children.

6. Programming should avoid appeals urging children to purchase the product specifically for the purpose of keeping the program on the air or which, for any reason, encourage children to enter inappropriate places.

7. Programming should present such subjects as violence and sex without undue emphasis and only as required by plot development or character delineation.

Violence, physical or psychological, should only be projected in responsibly handled contexts, not used to excess or exploitatively. Programs involving violence should present the consequences of it to its victims and perpetrators.

The depiction of conflict, and of material reflective of sexual considerations, when presented in programs designed primarily for children, should be handled with sensitivity.

8. The treatment of criminal activities should always convey their social and human effects.

The NAB Television Code

The following are some pertinent sections of the Television Code of the National Association of Broadcasters (Nineteenth Edition, June 1976). The code is a voluntary pledge which has been signed by many of the nation's television stations.

PROGRAM STANDARDS
I. Principles Governing Program Content

It is in the interest of television as a vital medium to encourage programs that are innovative, reflect a high degree of creative skill, deal with significant moral and social issues and present challenging concepts and other subject matter that relate to the world in which the viewer lives.

Television programs should not only reflect the influence of the established institutions that shape our values and culture, but also expose the dynamics of social change which bear upon our lives.

To achieve these goals, television broadcasters should be conversant with the general and specific needs, interests and aspirations of all the segments of the communities they serve. They should affirmatively seek out responsible representatives of all parts of their communities so that they may structure a broad range of programs that will inform, enlighten, and entertain the total audience.

Broadcasters should also develop programs directed toward advancing the cultural and educational aspects of their communities.

To assure that broadcasters have the freedom to program fully and responsibly, none of the provisions of this Code should be construed as preventing or impeding broadcast of the broad range of material necessary to help broadcasters fulfill their obligations to operate in the public interest.

The challenge to the broadcaster is to determine how suitably to present the complexities of human behavior. For televison, this requires exceptional awareness of considerations peculiar to the medium.

Accordingly, in selecting program subjects and themes, great care must be exercised to be sure that treatment and presentation are made in good faith and not for the purpose of sensationalism or to shock or exploit the audience or appeal to prurient interests or morbid curiosity.

Additionally, entertainment programming inappropriate for viewing by a general family audience should not be broadcast during the first hour of network entertainment programming in prime time and in the immediately preceding hour. In the occasional case when an entertainment program in this time period is deemed to be inappropriate for such an audience, advisories should be used to alert viewers. Advisories should also be used when programs in later prime time periods contain material that might be disturbing to significant segments of the audience.

These advisories should be presented in audio and video form at the beginning of the program and when deemed appropriate at a later point in the program. Advisories should also be used responsibly in promotional material in advance of the program. When using an advisory, the broadcaster should attempt to notify publishers of television program listings.

Special care should be taken with respect to the content and treatment of audience advisories so that they do not disserve their intended purpose by containing material that is promotional, sensational or exploitative. Promotional announcements for programs that include advisories should be scheduled on a basis consistent with the purpose of the advisory.

II. Responsibility Toward Children

Broadcasters have a special responsibility to children. Programs designed primarily for children should take into account the range of interests and needs of children from instructional and cultural material to a wide variety of entertainment material. In their totality, programs should contribute to the sound, balanced development of children to help them achieve a sense of the world at large and informed adjustments to their society.

In the course of a child's development, numerous social factors and forces, including television, affect the ability of the child to make the transition to adult society.

The child's training and experience during the formative years should include positive sets of values which will allow the child to become a responsible adult, capable of coping with the challenges of maturity.

Children should also be exposed, at the appropriate times, to a reasonable range of the realities which exist in the world sufficient to help them make the transition to adulthood.

Because children are allowed to watch programs designed primarily for adults, broadcasters should take this practice into account in the presentation of material in such programs when children may constitute a substantial segment of the audience.

All the standards set forth in this section apply to both program and commercial material designed and intended for viewing by children.

III. Community Responsibility

1. Television broadcasters and their staffs occupy positions of unique responsibility in their communities and should conscienti-

ously endeavor to be acquainted fully with the community's needs and characteristics in order better to serve the welfare of its citizens.

2. Requests for time for the placement of public service announcements or programs should be carefully reviewed with respect to the character and reputation of the group, compaign or organization involved, the public interest content of the message, and the manner of its presentation.

V. Treatment of News and Public Events

General

Television Code standards relating to the treatment of news and public events are, because of constitutional considerations, intended to be exhortatory. The standards set forth hereunder encourage high standards of professionalism in broadcast journalism. They are not to be interpreted as turning over to others the broadcaster's responsibility as to judgments necessary in news and public events programming.

News

1. A television station's news schedule should be adequate and well-balanced.

2. News reporting should be factual, fair and without bias.

3. A television broadcaster should exercise particular discrimination in the acceptance, placement and presentation of advertising in news programs so that such advertising should be clearly distinguishable from the news content.

4. At all times, pictorial and verbal material for both news and comment should conform to other sections of these standards, wherever such sections are reasonably applicable.

5. Good taste should prevail in the selection and handling of news:

Morbid, sensational or alarming details not essential to the factual report, especially in connection with stories of crime or sex, should be avoided. News should be telecast in such a manner as to avoid panic and unnecessary alarm.

6. Commentary and analysis should be clearly identified as such.

7. Pictorial material should be chosen with care and not presented in a misleading manner.

8. All news interview programs should be governed by accepted standards of ethical journalism, under which the interviewer selects the questions to be asked. Where there is advance agreement materially restricting an important or newsworthy area of questioning, the interviewer will state on the program that such limitation has been agreed upon. Such disclosure should be made if the person being interviewed requires that questions be submitted in advance or if he participates in editing a recording of the interview prior to its use on the air.

9. A television broadcaster should exercise due care in his supervision of content, format, and presentation of newscasts originated by his station, and in his selection of newscasters, commentators, and analysts.

Public Events

1. A television broadcaster has an affirmative responsibility at all times to be informed of public events, and to provide coverage consonant with the ends of an informed and enlightened citizenry.

2. The treatment of such events by a television broadcaster should provide adequate and informed coverage.

VI. Controversial Public Issues

1. Television provides a valuable forum for the expression of responsible views on public issues of a controversial nature. The television broadcaster should seek out and develop with accountable individuals, groups and organizations, programs relating to controversial public issues of import to his/her fellow citizens; and to give fair representation to opposing sides of issues which materially affect the life or welfare of a substantial segment of the public.

2. Requests by individuals, groups or organizations for time to discuss their views on controversial public issues should be considered on the basis of their individual merits, and in the light of the contribution which the use requested would make to the public interest, and to a well-balanced program structure.

3. Programs devoted to the discussion of controversial public issues should be identified as such. They should not be presented in

a manner which would mislead listeners or viewers to believe that the program is purely of an entertainment, news, or other character.

4. Broadcasts in which stations express their own opinions about issues of general public interest should be clearly identified as editorials. They should be unmistakably identified as statements of station opinion and should be appropriately distinguished from news and other program material.

VII. Political Telecasts

1. Political telecasts should be clearly identified as such. They should not be presented by a television broadcaster in a manner which would mislead listeners or viewers to believe that the program is of any other character.
(Ref.: Communications Act of 1934, as amended, Secs. 315 and 317, and FCC Rules and Regulations, Secs. 3.654, 3.657, 3.663, as discussed in NAB's "Political Broadcast Catechism & The Fairness Doctrine.")

VII. Religious Programs

1. It is the responsibility of a television broadcaster to make available to the community appropriate opportunity for religious presentations.

2. Programs reach audiences of all creeds simultaneously. Therefore, both the advocates of broad or ecumenical religious precepts, and the exponents of specific doctrines, are urged to present their positions in a manner conducive to viewer enlightenment on the role of religion in society.

3. In the allocation of time for telecasts of religious programs the television station should use its best efforts to apportion such time fairly among responsible individuals, groups and organizations.

Chapter 6
Editorializing

Editorializing is not universal among broadcast stations. There are two reasons. Historically, broadcasters were prohibited from editorializing during the early years of the medium's development. The other reason is a decision by some station licensees to avoid injecting themselves into controversy.

Editorializing occurs when the licensee or a duly authorized representative of the licensee takes a public stand on the air, stating the opinions expressed are those of the station or licensee.

While many worthwhile public affairs efforts can be undertaken by broadcast stations with a minimum of risk as far as criticism is concerned, a decision to editorialize means the licensee has decided to take a definite stand.

Frankly, the decision to editorialize means that someone in the audience will be offended by the station's decision. It also means the station's owners have made the decision to fulfill their natural role as a strong guiding force in the community.

The power of the mass media is readily acknowledged, and it seems to many that this power should be used firmly, with courage, to provide leadership rather than tossing it away solely for commercial gain.

Herein lies the inherent contradiction in commercial broadcasting. You are in business to make a profit, but the unique character of broadcasting in America sounds a call—legal and moral—for leadership in the community.

Time and again successful broadcasters have proven that they can provide a well-rounded community service and operate a profitable business at the same time.

A BRIEF HISTORY OF EDITORIALIZING

The history of American broadcasting has been filled with stories of the vigorous battles between the written press and broadcasters. One of the longest battles was over the origination of news from radio stations. Another long battle took place over the issue of editorializing.

A few station operators realized that they could enhance their prestige and position in the community by becoming catalysts for public opinion. This was a role which had been the exclusive domain of newspapers and a few magazines.

The year was 1941, and Radio Station WAAB (then in Boston) applied for renewal of its license. The station had been airing editorials in which it supported various candidates for public office. In addition, the station had taken stands on a number of public issues.

The Federal Communications Commission delivered a shocker. It told WAAB its license would be renewed, but WAAB would have to stop editorializing.

The decision became known as the "Mayflower Decision," getting its name from the Mayflower Broadcasting Corporation which had applied for the frequency occupied by WAAB.

The Commission ruling said, in part: "A truly free radio cannot be used to advocate the causes of the licensee. It cannot be used to support the candidacies of his friends. It cannot be devoted to the support of principles he happens to regard most favorably. In brief, the broadcaster cannot be an advocate."

The Commission held that it was not in the public interest—recalling the cornerstone phrase of the Communications Act of 1934: "Public interest, convenience and necessity"—for broadcasters to editorialize.

The broadcaster cannot be an advocate—a true sword of Damocles, dangling over an industry which was just beginning to flex its "freedom of press" muscles.

+ In re The Yankee Network, Inc., 8 FCC 333 at 340 (1941).

World War II arrived and along with accepting voluntary censorship, the broadcast industry chose not to challenge the Mayflower decision until the end of the war.

Then, the National Association of Broadcasters tackled the challenge and, finally, on July 1, 1949, the FCC reversed the Mayflower decision, ruling that broadcast stations could editorialize if they maintained balance of differing opinions on an issue. The report, which noted this reversal of policy, introduced what has become known as the Fairness Doctrine.

Ironically, in saying that stations could advocate, the FCC went a good distance in the opposite direction from the Mayflower decision, saying that stations had a duty to discuss controversial issues.

The key to the new approach was the word "fairness." The Commission directed that a licensee must make his "facilities available for expression of contrasting points of view, of all responsible elements in the community on the various issues which arise..."

The Fairness Doctrine makes it the responsibility of the licensee to devote what the FCC calls a "reasonable percentage" of a station's broadcast time to the discussion of public issues of interest to the community served by the station. The clincher is contained in this excerpt from the Doctrine:

> We do not believe, however, that the licensee's obligation to serve the public interest can be met merely through the adoption of a general policy of not refusing to broadcast opposing views where a demand is made of the station for broadcast time...Broadcast licensees have an affirmative duty generally to encourage and implement the broadcast of all sides of controversial issues over their facilities.

This does not mean that a station HAS to editorialize, but it does indicate plenty of latitude to do so; and it certainly makes sense to do so as part of a station's overall public affairs programming.

Look for the catch words in the preceding excerpt: They are "affirmative duty," meaning that a station must do more than just throw open the doors to the expression of various sentiments. It must positively seek out a variety of expressions on issues of community concern. We've already mentioned the role of the FCC's ascertainment policy in this seeking-out process.

And, in the case of editorials, there is one more consideration. There is an aspect of the Fairness Doctrine called the "personal attack rule" which must be observed in airing editorials. Essentially, if you air a personal attack against an individual in an editorial you must positively seek out that individual and offer free (and equivalent) time for reply.

The Personal Attack Rule applies to more than editorials. It also applies to commentary, documentaries and some programs. Specifically exempt are newscasts, news interviews and on-the-spot coverage of news events.

HANDLING CONTRASTING VIEWS

Any station which plans to editorialize should think out a defined procedure and policy and stick to it. For instance, the policy should state who writes and who airs editorials. Usually editorials are aired by the person who speaks for the licensee, frequently the station manager, but it might be an editorial director or even the news director.

Many in the industry feel that news directors should be involved in the planning and perhaps the writing of editorials, but should not air them because the audience can become confused as to when the news director is an unbiased reporter, and when the news director is voicing an opinion. This is less of a problem in a station where the news director is primarily an administrator and is not seen or heard on the air, except as an editorialist.

All in all, it's better if the news director does not air editorials.

Most stations establish some type of editorial board, so that viewpoints to be written into station editorials can be tossed around among a group of people within the station who understand the community's needs. Frequently, the editorial board is the station's management team, but it may be expanded to include staff or supervisory personnel who might not otherwise participate in top management decisions.

In a small radio or television station, the process of discussing editorial stands may be highly informal. In larger stations, there may be structured meetings of the editorial board with minutes kept for the files.

Another troublesome policy area is how to handle the positive obligation to solicit replies. First, every editorial should end with a clear statement that the station welcomes comments from members of the audience. The station does not have to put itself on record as being willing to broadcast all comments received, but it should carefully study all responses to determine, if the persons calling or writing do represent alternative points of view which warrant expression.

If so, these persons should be notified that air time is available, and they should be offered whatever assistance is needed in getting their editorial replies on the air. It must not be forgotten that a person replying to an editorial does not necessarily need to belong to or represent a particular group. An individual citizen—who, in the opinion of station management, speaks for a segment of public opinion, should have the opportunity of replying to an editorial.

The station should establish a defined procedure for seeking out spokespersons for contrasting viewpoints. The first way to do this is to make lists of key leaders in the community (and keep these lists up to date). Depending on the size of the community, you may want to break these lists into categories such as political and governmental, educational, business, health, civic, social, etc. If it is financially feasible, the station should mail copies of each editorial to some or all of the list .

The station should always have copies of the editorial available for mailing on request and should always send copies to individuals or groups directly affected by the content of the editorial.

Under FCC rules, if the editorial contains a personal attack, the transcript of the editorial must be delivered promptly to the individual attacked and must be accompanied by a positive offer of time for rebuttal. In no case can the notification be made later than seven days after the broadcast. The copy of the editorial may be either a transcript or a tape.

The obligation to positively seek out other viewpoints does not end with the on-air offer to accept comments, or the mailing of transcripts to names on a mailing list. The station is obliged under the Fairness Doctrine to specifically contact individuals or groups who can be expected to be interested in the content of the editorial.

Here's an example: Your station is preparing an editorial which opposes construction of a new county jail. The editorial ends with the customary statement that the station welcomes comments from members of the public. You will routinely mail or deliver copies of the editorial to the appointed and elected leaders of the municipal and county governments in the affected county, plus the top law enforcement officials and the local judiciary.

To meet your obligation completely, you should be certain to contact the local bar association, any groups which take an interest in prisoner rights or public expenditures, the American Civil Liberties Union, the Fortune Society (which is made up of ex-offenders), local or state groups which conduct studies of corrections systems (such as the League of Women Voters), the chamber of commerce, the government institute at the State University, probation, parole and correction associations, the appropriate unions, and the appropriate police associations.

The FCC in reversing the Mayflower decision and in developing the Fairness Doctrine has placed a heavy burden on stations. The decision to air editorials makes this burden heavier, but the Fairness obligation exists for all public affairs programming, whether or not the station chooses to editorialize.

Out of the total number of stations which editorialize, a much smaller proportion go as far as advocating the condidacy of specific political office seekers. Stations which do not endorse candidates, cite among their reasons a desire to not become embroiled in the heat of local politics.

One station owner, Mrs. Betty Ramey of WRKL in Rockland County, New York says she does not do political editorials, because hers is the only station actually located in Rockland County, thus there is no other outlet for a contrasting viewpoint. Obviously she ignores the print media in taking this stand. She could cover opposing viewpoints simply by soliciting those views and making editorial time available for replies.

Bill O'Shaughnessy of WVOX in nearby Westchester County, New York does air political endorsements. He makes a policy of keeping them to himself until air time, and then, says O'Shaughnessy: "...with the political editorials I get the fastest...taxi driver here, and I get him to go across the town and deliver it the minute the editorial goes on the air."

O'Shaugnessy admits his political endorsements have gotten him into hot water on occasions, but he also speaks in favor of stirring the pot when it comes to discussing local issues. WVOX is healthy financially—station managers in more marginal situations have a tendency to tread a little less boldly.

It is essential that the station which endorses a political candidate move quickly and effectively to offer the opposing candidates an opportunity to respond. It is a good idea to extend this policy to include persons designated by the candidates to speak for them, a fact that should be clearly deliniated in the introduction and closing which wraps around the editorial reply.

Because the Fairness Doctrine is involved in all editorializing, a station's management must be certain that it keeps files of all editorials and replies, including the days, dates and times aired, and transcripts or tapes of the editorials themselves. All correspondence or notes on phone calls related to editorials—notifications, requests for replies, etc.—should also be on file.

If editorials are mailed out, there should be notations as to whom the transcripts were sent and when. And files relating to any personal attacks should be kept separate and in addition to regular editorial files. The care with which these records are kept becomes extremely important at renewal time—especially if any challenges are filed against the application.

In 1976 the broadcast industry was rocked by the WHAR case, which has a direct bearing on the question of fairness.

WHAR (AM) is located in Clarksburg, West Virginia in strip-mining country. Strip-mining, which involves the taking off of the surface of the land to reach coal just beneath the surface, has been highly controversial. The coal and energy industries defend the practice as an economical way of mining coal. Environmentalists contend that the method leaves the land wasted and the water supplies poisoned.

Acting on a complaint filed against the station, the FCC told WHAR that it had violated the Fairness Doctrine through the station's alleged failure to cover the strip-mining issue adequately.

The complaint was filed by the Media Access Project on behalf of Democratic Congresswoman Patsy Mink of Hawaii. The action was joined by the Environmental Policy Center and O.D. Hagedorn, a resident of Clarksburg.

Congresswoman Mink had sponsored an anti-strip-mining bill. In July, 1974 she wrote WHAR and other stations seeking air time for an eleven-minute tape in which she explained her proposal. The tape was prepared, Congresswoman Mink claimed, to contrast a program prepared by the U.S. Chamber of Commerce which she claimed was in favor of strip-mining.

WHAR returned the Mink tape saying it had not aired the Chamber of Commerce tape either.

The station had claimed it presented "a significant amount of information" on the strip-mining issue, but none of the programming was locally produced. The station also failed to provide documentation for the programming it claimed to have presented.

Observers of FCC workings say the Commission is usually willing to take rather sketchy evidence of compliance from a station, and then issue a letter urging better compliance. However, in the WHAR case the Commission felt it could not ignore the fact that the station could not document, clearly, the specific programs it had broadcast on the strip-mining issue.

The FCC directed the station to state how it would remedy this apparent lack of local discussion over its facility on the strip-mining issue.

One FCC Commissioner, Glen O. Robinson, later issued a statement that he does not interpret the FCC order to WHAR as meaning a station has to originate local programming on an issue to meet its Fairness Doctrine obligations. In the case of WHAR, the station wasn't able to document wire service or network stories it claimed to have carried.

Industry observers are worried about the WHAR decision. It could set a precedent, with interest groups assailing stations for not covering issues, and the FCC subsequently telling stations what they should program—a role the FCC has tried to avoid, since the Communications Act prohibits the Commission from censoring the programming of licensees.

Other observers feel that the circumstances of the WHAR situation were so individualistic that the case will not set a precedent.

It would be unrealistic to think the WHAR case did not set some sort of precedent. It is only natural that concerned interest groups will use the WHAR precedent in their assults on what they believe to be recalcitrant members of the broadcast media. And the FCC will be called on to decide, again, if it should take an action regarding an individual station's programming.

Broadcasters should not forget that they now have sets of rules to comply with which virtually demand local programming on controversial issues. The first is the Fairness Doctrine which makes two demands: (1) a station must cover controversial issues of public importance and; (2) broadcasters must deal with these issues in a balanced way.

The second set of rules is the FCC's ascertainment policy, which requires the station to define in writing the important issues affecting the community. Thus the station has to document the very issues which then become input for the fairness test, if the licensee is challenged.

It's reasonable to expect that a station could be asked to explain how it failed to discover a need or issue, if an interest group can demonstrate that the issue exists within the fabric of the community.

There is no reason for a station to ignore community issues. To do so is to pursue the greedy, profit-only orientation which has given broadcasting a black eye since its inception. Most of the current interference by the FCC results from the abdication of responsibility by licensees, who apparently would rather run the risk of government meddling than assume the responsibility for serving their communities.

It's true that it may take more courage—and entails greater risks—to involve a station in controversy in some communities. It's easy enough to visualize the challenges facing a station owner in an economically-marginal, coal mining community compared to the challenges faced by a station owner in a vital, industrially diversified community. But the writing is on the wall, and it behooves broadcasters to do the best they can to be an important part of the life and thought of their communities.

Community involvement means much more than the airing of community issues. It means the support and development of the community's economy, recreational facilities, schools, churches, cultural resources and other essential ingredients of a "good place to live."

HOW VARIOUS STATIONS EDITORIALIZE

For the most part, editorial formats are fairly consistent from station to station. If you were to listen to or view the typical broadcast station, you could expect a few introductory words stating that "the following is an XXXX editorial, presented by J. Throckmor-

139

ton Waxingeloquent." The body of the editorial would follow, trailed by an announcement restating that station XXXX had just presented an editorial and comments are welcome from persons or groups having contrasting views. A copy of this editorial can be obtained by phoning or writing XXXX"

Simple, clean and effective, But, as we shall discover, only one way to do an editorial.

The rather structured open and close is designed to clearly set the editorial apart from other programming, and to meet certain FCC guidelines about contrasting viewpoints. This framework is especially important for stations which place editorials adjacent to newscasts. It is essential to make clear that the expression of opinion contained in the editorial is separate from the unbiased content of the newscast.

Some radio stations use more flexible presentations, either to fit their formats or to meet the practical requirements of time and facilities.

WRKL

Mrs. Betty Ramey of WRKL in Rockland County, New York does some of her editorials at the opening of the station's six-day-a-week, telephone-talk show. This sort of editorial is done only on the show. Mrs. Ramey opens the program by delivering her editorial, and then frequently moves on to interview or solicit comment from a studio guest who is either affected by the editorial's content or who holds a contrasting viewpoint. Finally, the listening audience is invited to call in and comment on the matter under discussion.

WRKL also airs the traditional, pre-recorded editorial which is usually scheduled to follow a newscast.

Mrs. Ramey said that, generally speaking, WRKL editorials are aimed at local rather than national and international subjects. "I feel," said Mrs. Ramey, "that those issues which we treat in detail should have local involvement."

WSME

General Manager Charlie Smith of WSME in Sanford, Maine prepares and delivers his station's editorials. Smith said: "I consult with our news director and try and be sure that I'm fully aware of everything that's going on on an issue before I take a position on it. We write all our material ourselves and our editorials tend not to be daily things, but we try to have at least a couple a week and to have them be sensible...you know, something heralding the coming of spring and that type of thing you tend to see in our weekly newspaper seems kind of useless to me. When we do an editorial we try to be topical and to say something and at least start people thinking about what we're talking about."

Smith also has some thoughts on the risks facing a small market station when it does editorials. "I think that on a number of occasions we've taken some fairly strong positions and not necessarily popular ones. And naturally, as a small station, there's some trepidation when you go into this 'what if our sponsors come in and cancel after I gore their particular ox?'. But we've found a positive reaction to the fact that the station is coming out and taking positions."

WSME saves the typed-out text of all editorials but does not mail them out from a mailing list. Smith explained, "the topics we're editorializing on are local ones and we are in contact with the established groups and potential respondents on a day-to-day basis...inviting them to come on...most of these people are trying to ignore any criticism that might be made whether it is by us or the newspaper or any other group." Smith points out that one problem he sees is the people who represent valid opinions, but who aren't in positions in established groups where they would receive the mailed editorials. For this reason Smith is particularly pleased when his on-air appeal for responses results in his receiving a letter or phone call.

WDAE

WDAE in Tampa, Florida editorialized two or three times a week. Depending on the state of the economy, the station has employed an editorial writer whose sole responsibility was the researching and writing of editorials for airing by the general manager. Tampa is a large market, and it can be financially feasible for a radio station in a market the size of Tampa to hire an editorial specialist. Generally, you find most editorial writers are employed by television stations.

Former WDAE General Manager Don Clark advocates doing editorials when you have something to say, rather than meeting a specific quota in terms of so many days per week or a total number of editorials. Clark said: "We do not sit down and say alright now, you have to have an editorial today or have to have an editorial every Wednesday....to me that would steal away from the importance of it. We come out on subjects that people are talking about or very interested in, but may not have the benefit of the research that we do on it."

Clark is an advocate of broadcast editorials, saying that there are many issues which require a station to express an opinion or interpret what it feels is the truth, neither of which are proper functions of the regular newscasts.

Clark also advocates informing an individual who is the target of an editorial in advance, and then running that person's reply adjacent to the editorial, rather than expecting members of the audience to recall what was said on some earlier occasion.

WCBS-TV

Peter Kohler is the editorial director of WCBS-TV in New York City. He is also a past-president of the National Broadcast Editorial Association and one of the nation's most experienced editorialists.

Kohler described the role of the editorial writer: "...what you're trying to do is get people to think about issues...more than we try to go out and stampede their legislators for one reason or another. Human behavior just seems to me is not moved by lecturer or being implored to do things."

What if you have just been named the editorial director? Kohler had some thoughts: "I think the best thing for a starting editorial writer is to not suddenly think someone has recognized your inate intelligence to be able to be a problem solver for all things. I think the best background for an editorial writer is basically reporting. Editorial writers who suddenly take on that job and give up the reporting end of it aren't going to be very good at it.

"I think you quickly find out that on most subjects somebody else knows more about it than you do, and the only way that you can competently deal with it is to talk with the people who do know. It brings you into a kind of reporting that I find is kind of fun, but very different from your usual news reporting in the sense that you're almost entirely working off record or 'background only.' You try to get to people who are close to the subject and who are involved in trying to settle it or resolve it one way or the other..."

WCBS-TV has a full-fledged editorial department, headed by Kohler, with an associate, an editorial producer, a part-time secretary and student interns.

The station does six editorials or replies a week. The editorials are written by Kohler or his associate, or, on occasion, by the producer. Each department member has certain specialities, and editorials are frequently prepared by the person with the specialized knowledge, once it's determined what topics will be covered. WCBS-TV has found that about one-third of its total editorial time is devoted to editorial replies. This is a high percentage, based on reports from other stations, and probably reflects the media sophistication of civic leaders and viewers in the New York metropolitan area.

The station pays a great deal of attention to visuals. As Kohler said: "If a highway is going to cut through this part of the countryside—and it's a nice piece of countryside and we don't want it to do that—there's no better way, just go out there, do a stand-up...and walk around and show people what it looks like. It's that kind of let's show 'em what it looks like or let's show 'em the problem where it really pertains.

"We did an editorial about people in New Jersey wanting to get to the Statue of Liberty which you can throw a rock at it, but you can't get there because there's no service between Jersey City, Bayonne, places like that and the Statue of Liberty." WCBS-TV then took its viewers through the tortuous route New Jersey residents must take by—for instance—by bus, train, subway and boat to reach their famous neighbor.

Quality is important. Kohler said WCBS likes to produce visually—in graphics—up to its local news standard.

Another technique used by WCBS-TV is to show a slide of someone's face at the opening of a studio editorial. Kohler said having a picture available helps the editorial writer. "I think that helps you write about a person—it's very easy to take issues away from being about people, but usually an issue is identified with a person and when, I think, that human being's name is written into the piece it takes on more vigor."

WXII-TV

In Piedmont, North Carolina, WXII-TV editorializes sporatically, depending on the issues and the time the general manager has available to write the editorial. The topics are local and statewide, and copies are sent to both a regular mailing list and people who might be interested in replying.

WDBJ-TV

Nearby, at WDBJ-TV in Roanoke, Virginia, Ted Powers presides over the editorial writing. He has a firm opinion on what differentiates an editorial from news analysis or opinion. Powers uses a three-point yardstick:

An editorial must contain:

1. A statement of what the issue on contention is.
2. A conclusion on the part of the editorialist (management's stand).
3. A suggestion that the viewer take some action. (Write your congressman, mayor, city councilman; attend a meeting of some civic body and voice your views, etc.)

Powers, also a president of the National Broadcast Editorial Association, has his own theory on visuals for television editorials: "There are those who feel that since our visual impact is so great,...every editorial should have film or videotape to back it up and...the editorialist should be on-screen only briefly. Maybe they're right, but I have observed that many stations, in their effort to make it visual, forget the salient point of the editorial as they strive for visual impact...I think the key to an editorial on television, as in a newspaper or on radio, is the content and quality of the writing."

Many stations, especially televisions stations, decide the subjects for their editorials during meetings of their editorial board. Powers had some thoughts on this particular editorial structure: "One of the largest hindrances to forceful and forthright TV editorials is the over-large 'editorial board.' I know of many stations which have 10-or-more-member editorial boards. The only consensus that is usually possible among such a large number of people is that they are 'for God and Motherhood,' and 'against sin.' "

Powers continued: "It is my feeling that an editorial board should consist of 3, or at the most 4, people. These should be the station manager, the editorialist, the news director and/or the public affairs director. They should meet at regularly scheduled times

..Having decided on the subject matter, the station manager (who bears the final responsibility for what's on the station's air) must decide the editorial's position. The editorialist then writes the piece, runs it by the rest of the board for comment, sets the final copy and it goes on air."

WGAN-TV

Charles Sanford, vice-president of WGAN-TV in Portland, Maine said his station averages three editorials a month. The precise schedule is determined by the issues which arise. WGAN uses the editorial board concept, with the board consisting of Sanford, the managers of WGAN radio and television, and the radio and TV news directors.

One thing which concerns Sanford is editorial replies. He reports that replies average about one-quarter of the total number of editorials broadcast. Sanford says, frequently, WGAN will do an editorial on an issue on which there is a great deal of interest and consequently, will get a number of letters and telephone calls. However, when the time comes for the respondents to actually prepare a script and record their reply, they tend to just fade away. Sanford says his station tries to offset the problem by going out and seeking responses, but this has only a slight effect in raising the total number of responses.

KGO-TV

KGO is located in San Francisco. The station believes in using visuals where they are appropriate. One project, which attracted national attention among editorial writers, was a group of three editorials done over a two-year period which attacked the problem of Doyle Drive, a dangerous approach to the famed Golden Gate Bridge.

It seemed only logical to go out and do the editorial on location, and that's precisely what the station did (Fig. 6-1).

PREPARING THE EDITORIAL

The single biggest drawback to doing editorials is the fear of tackling the job. Some station managers actively fear what they see as a massive research task.

Fig. 6-1. The General Manager of KGO-TV, San Francisco doing an on-scene editorial concerning a dangerous approach to the Golden Gate Bridge. (Photo courtesy of KGO-TV).

As in any endeavor, think in terms of your limitations when you think about editorializing.

Station resources are your first consideration. But think of other factors. As Charlie Smith of WSME in Sanford, Maine pointed out earlier in this chapter, a small station in a small market has day to day familiarity with issues and personalities, which can make up for the lack of an editorial writer and fancy research facilities. It just plain isn't that difficult to do a good editorial on the future of the town dump, if you've been around a community for a while.

The general manager and the news director probably both attend public meetings. They both know the newsmakers personally and know the issues under discussion in town, as well as who represents what viewpoint. And, if they've been doing their jobs, the manager and news director have already discussed current views on important issues with these people.

So, in many cases it's just a matter of sitting down and thinking—and perhaps discussing with the staff—different approaches to community problems. You then decide on what sort of stand you want to take. Often what is needed more than anything else is a list of the pros and cons of the issue, so the audience can make up their own minds.

When a general manager sits down to outline an editorial, he or she becomes increasingly aware of just how valuable a good news director can be. The news director is apt to be better informed on more aspects of a community issue than even the general manager. Also, the general manager and news director travel in different social and political circles, so there may be a broadening of available information through a sharing of ideas.

A good news director is skilled at quick research, calling the right people to elicit essential facts. A good news director knows the people at the federal, state and local level who can provide data; he or she knows how the local college can help, and who really moves and shakes the community. No matter what the size or economic strength of a station, if you plan to do the best job you can in news...public affairs...and editorials...hire the best news director you can recruit and afford. If you have more money, go out and augment your staff with a public affairs and/or editorial specialist.

Your station should have a simple filing system to help in researching editorials. First of all, the news department should keep clipping files—containing press releases, newspaper clips, old scripts and wire copy on the key topics of continuing concern. Reporters may add to this file by inserting documents they pick up, or copies of their notes and scripts. Someone should be designed to make certain the file is kept up to date and is augmented by other valuable scraps of data such as publications, clippings from other sources, reports and documents.

To supplement the files, the station should have some factual reference books, such as the appropriate state manual which lists legislative committees, various state and county departments and the like; a congressional directory; a couple of almanacs; a good dictionary and every free directory which comes in the door. (For instance, when the American Bar Association sends you its directory, don't throw it away, put it on the reference shelf.)

Most of these reference books are free for the asking. You should also have copies of current municipal and county budgets, and of the major studies and reports which are likely to pop up in current controversies.

Peter Kohler of WCBS-TV has these thoughts on research: "I think, basically, in an editorial operation you can take a little more time to gather it [information] so, if it's not all at your fingertips, you don't have to feel that you have to...not do it...There are some fundamental elements that are part of anybody's basic library...not that hard to come by and any station that is in the business of presenting news...ought to have...things like Congressional Quarterly or some service like that or National Journal...depending on what states they are in they ought to have lots of newspapers coming in. If their town is not in the state capital, they ought to get the state capital newspaper, the best one they can find."

Kohler had another suggestion: "Check what committees your congressmen and senators are on...their committee staffs will deluge you with resource material—not policy—just resource material."

Let's say that you hit on a topic which requires a little more sophisticated sort of research. Perhaps you will find some outside organization which can help. One starting point is the public library. Then check the libraries at your local colleges and universities or the state library.

If your station is affiliated with a network, it may be that the network's news division has a fine reference library which might be willing to help you.

And there are numerous organizations which will put together data—some of which will be self-serving—such as the Better Business Bureau, the Chamber of Commerce, the League of Women Voters, the Wilderness Society, the bar and medical associations, labor unions, churches and groups which conduct lobbying or public affairs activities.

In writing an editorial, remember that the cardinal rule is SIMPLICITY. Try to convey one idea and one idea only. If you oppose expansion of the local transit district, don't go off on a tangent discussing the Federal Highway Trust Fund. Tell us why you think the proposed expansion of the transit district is unwise, and then tell us what action we should take. Should we vote against a bond issue, or should we attend an upcoming public hearing?

Don't dazzle us with figures and quotes...use plain language, tell the story as simply as you can and end with an appeal to do something.

There's a good question about whether there is any point to doing an editorial which does not urge some type of active response.

There are exceptions, of course. Once in a great while there comes a time when you will do a laudatory or memorial editorial—because you have something to say about an individual that cannot be said as well elsewhere. These occasions are made important by the fact that they occur only rarely.

But, in all other cases, what we would like to do is get our audience talking about community problems.

There's an old saying about writing speeches: "Tell 'em what you're going to tell 'em—tell 'em—tell 'em you told 'em."

It applies to editorials. In the few words you have, 100 to 300 being typical, tell the audience what you're going to talk about, expand and elaborate on your topic, and tell them what you said—followed by an appeal for thought or, better yet, action.

Don't ignore the fact that life has a lighter side. Once in a while do an essay on the brighter side of life. Only don't make it the staple diet of your editorials.

PRODUCTION

The amazing thing about the development of broadcast editorials is that it has taken so long for broadcasters to recognize that an editorial need not be a verbal copy of a newspaper editorial.

Today clever, creative stations are putting sound and pictures into their editorials. For example, why quote civic leaders when your news department has them on tape? Go back in your files, get the tape excerpts and put them in the editorial. If a local political leader has gone back on his campaign promise, put your tape of him making the promise into the editorial. Let civic leaders speak for themselves.

If you want to remind us of Franklin Delano Roosevelt's words …then if you have him on disc or tape…insert a sound bite in your editorial.

If music or sound effect are appropriate—use them. For instance—you're complaining about the level of noise in a certain area of town. Go out and tape the noise—if it is recognizeable on tape, or on film—then demonstrate what you're talking about by putting audio or video into your editorial.

You've decided to do an editorial on prayer in the public schools. So go out and film or record children reciting prayers in the public schools.

You want to attack the quality of street cleaning in your city. Go out and shoot film or tape of the conditions, you think should be cleaned up. Show your audience what you are talking about!

One television station in New York City aired an editorial which was shot on film in the community where the conditions being discussed existed. Local people were shown, and heard, discussing their problems. Then the editorialist appeared on the screen to summarize and state the station's viewpoint—followed by an appeal for action.

Editorial writing is not a monster. Know what you want to say, then discuss the issue clearly in plain language and use sound or pictures to help you, if they will improve the quality of the message.

SUMMARY

Editorializing is an excellent device for the station which wants to stand above its competition, and be recognized as a leader in the community.

Like anyone who has the strength of his convictions, the station and its management will be subjected to comment and criticism, but the experience of most aggressive editorializing stations is that, in the long run, the community becomes more involved in the station just because it does take stands. People will know you exist!

One community broadcaster believes that his radio station belongs to the community. He tells everyone who will listen that the station is *their* station. And he knows that his editorials stir comments—because he's seen and heard them. His approach has paid off handsomely in public involvement, professional recognition and revenues.

Peter Kohler has a few words which are worth remembering: "Don't think that suddenly you've been exalted to a position where now whatever you think or whatever strikes you as interesting in judgment is valid. You've got to still do the reporting, perhaps in a different way and perhaps more vigorously than you did it before..."

Once you have decided to editorialize—don't compromise. Stand for something—for something important in your particular community. Don't attack the highway safety problem nationwide—tell your audience how the beltway around your town can be improved to put a stop to the terrible pileups that occur every winter.

Keep your editorials in their place. Make certain that nothing about your presentation—the placement or the presenter—confuses your audience, as to where unbiased balanced news coverage ends and statements of station opinion begin.

Seriously consider whether your station can make a little hole in the budget for an editorial director or a combined editorial and public affairs' director. This will provide quality, continuity and guidance to your total public affairs effort.

Be creative. Sell a good idea in an editorial with the same skill you sell a product or service idea in a commercial. Get the audience's attention, and then stimulate them to go do something about community problems.

Keep records—do a good job and be ready to document it—it's the best insurance you can buy for your FCC license!

At the end of this chapter, we are including some samples of editorials actually broadcast on selected radio and television stations:

DOYLE DRIVE

We, in the Bay Area, often boast about our cultural and humane approach to life But perhaps, we should begin to question this presumption, in the light of our demonstrated priorities. Events seem to indicate we care much more about animal life than we do about human life. An oil spill brings hundreds of citizens out to clean up the birds, it brings lawsuits, and it brings cries for stricter laws and stiffer penalties. Fine. But one finds a strange lack of public uproar and concern about situations that provide a constant danger to human lives. Birds we take great pains to clean and protect, but humans we seem to neglect and often let die. The Doyle Drive approach to the Golden Gate Bridge has been the scene and cause of fatal and near fatal accidents for years. There have been 19 head-on collisions there since 1966, 409 accidents in the past 5 years, a ten-death accident in 1970, and a two-death accident last month. It is a six-lane, undivided death trap We know that unless immediate and effective action is taken to widen and separate it, more people will be injured or killed on it. For years now, the Golden Gate Bridge District, the San Francisco Board of Supervisors, and other public bodies have been begging the State Highway Commission to bring Doyle Drive up to freeway standards for safety. Yet the Commission says it will not fund such an effort until fiscal year 1976-77. That's not nearly good enough if you value human life at all. We want action taken on Doyle Drive now If you agree, why not write Governor Reagan and your California legislators in Sacramento and urge the immediate passage of the Foran and Marks bills which would make Doyle Drive safe.

VARIOUS TIMES:
February 14, 1973-February 17, 1973
Time: 1:55
VTR 718-2156

KGO-TV. 277 GOLDEN GATE AVENUE. SAN FRANCISCO. CALIFORNIA 94102. (415) 863-0077
AN ABC OWNED TELEVISION STATION

KGO -TV regularly presents editorials on topics of vital interest to its viewers.
Clearly labeled as opinion, these television editorials are delivered by KGO -TV Vice President and General Manager, Russ C. Coughlan.
Your comments concerning the attached editorial will be greatly appreciated.
Robert A. Sunderland, Editorial Director

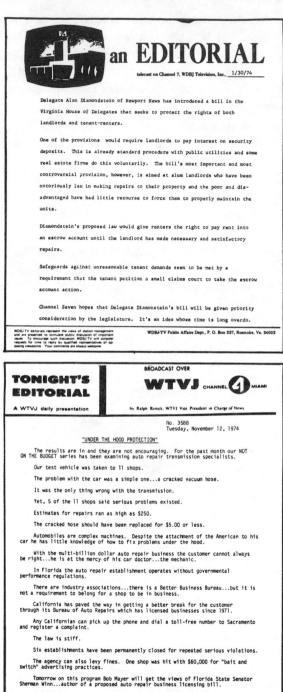

an EDITORIAL

telecast on Channel 7, WDBJ Television, Inc., 1/30/74

Delegate Alan Diamondstein of Newport News has introduced a bill in the
Virginia House of Delegates that seeks to protect the rights of both
landlords and tenant-renters.

One of the provisions would require landlords to pay interest on security
deposits. This is already standard procedure with public utilities and some
real estate firms do this voluntarily. The bill's most important and most
controversial provision, however, is aimed at slum landlords who have been
notoriously lax in making repairs to their property and the poor and disadvantaged have had little recourse to force them to properly maintain the
units.

Diamondstein's proposed law would give renters the right to pay rent into
an escrow account until the landlord has made necessary and satisfactory
repairs.

Safeguards against unreasonable tenant demands seem to be met by a
requirement that the tenant petition a small claims court to take the escrow
account action.

Channel Seven hopes that Delegate Diamonstein's bill will be given priority
consideration by the legislature. It's an idea whose time is long overdo.

WDBJ TV editorials represent the views of station management and are presented to stimulate public discussion of important issues. To encourage such discussion, WDBJ TV will consider requests for time to reply by qualified representatives of opposing viewpoints. Your comments are always welcome.

WDBJ-TV Public Affairs Dept., P. O. Box 227, Roanoke, Va. 24002

TONIGHT'S EDITORIAL

A WTVJ daily presentation

BROADCAST OVER

WTVJ CHANNEL 4 MIAMI

by Ralph Renick, WTVJ Vice President in Charge of News

No. 3588
Tuesday, November 12, 1974

"UNDER THE HOOD PROTECTION"

The results are in and they are not encouraging. For the past month our NOT
ON THE BUDGET series has been examining auto repair transmission specialists.

Our test vehicle was taken to 11 shops.

The problem with the car was a simple one...a cracked vacuum hose.

It was the only thing wrong with the transmission.

Yet, 5 of the 11 shops said serious problems existed.

Estimates for repairs ran as high as $250.

The cracked hose should have been replaced for $5.00 or less.

Automobiles are complex machines. Despite the attachment of the American to his
car he has little knowledge of how to fix problems under the hood.

With the multi-billion dollar auto repair business the customer cannot always
be right...he is at the mercy of his car doctor...the mechanic.

In Florida the auto repair establishment operates without governmental
performance regulations.

There are industry associations...there is a Better Business Bureau...but it is
not a requirement to belong for a shop to be in business.

California has paved the way in getting a better break for the customer
through its Bureau of Auto Repairs which has licensed businesses since 1971.

Any Californian can pick up the phone and dial a toll-free number to Sacramento
and register a complaint.

The law is stiff.

Six establishments have been permanently closed for repeated serious violations.

The agency can also levy fines. One shop was hit with $60,000 for "bait and
switch" advertising practices.

Tomorrow on this program Bob Mayer will get the views of Florida State Senator
Sherman Winn...author of a proposed auto repair business licensing bill.

It is one of those needed pieces of legislation which honest operators should
welcome along with the guy whose transmission vacuum hose goes on the fritz.

Chapter 7
Political Broadcasts

Broadcasting is unique within our communications system because it enjoys some of the freedoms of the press, and yet must abide by a multitude of government regulations.

One of the areas in which there has been the greatest interference by the government is in the programming of political material—editorials, debates, political commercials.

We will take a look at the regulations affecting public affairs programming in this chapter.

THE REGULATIONS

Broadcasting gets its basic regulatory framework from the Communications Act of 1934. The Act has certain specific sections which pertain directly to the public affairs programming of radio and TV stations.

First, the Act refers to broadcasting as something which is done in the "public interest, convenience and necessity." The phrase traces its history back to public utility legislation and has been a constant burden to broadcasters and the Federal Communications Commission alike.

What is the public interest, convenience and necessity? This is the question with which the FCC has been struggling ever since the Communications Act was passed.

The phrase appears a number of times in the text of the Communications Act. It is applied to several functions delegated to the FCC including the regulation of stations as to location, frequency, power and technical facilities. The Commission can, in the public interest, convenience and necessity, do things like setting license qualifications and require the keeping of certain records.

The end result is that the FCC has ample latitude within the Communications Act to use its discretion in making regulations. In a 1946 court case, it was pointed out that the Commission may not act capriciously. It must hold hearings and seek opinions before taking either policy actions or acting on the licenses of specific stations.

The court also admitted that it would be difficult, if not impossible, to provide a precise definition of the operative phrase "public interest, convenience and necessity."

The one major prohibition in the Act is that the Commission cannot censor a station's broadcasts. However, while the Commission cannot censor a station's broadcasts prior to transmission, the Commission can hold a station responsible following the broadcast—either through the renewal process, or by asking a station to respond to a specific complaint on file with the Commission. It is censorship through implied threat. A cautious station owner begins to think in terms of what the Commission might question.

The FCC is allowed to interfere in certain specific matters, such as the broadcast of obscenity or in certain advertising practices, and in broadcasts which present a clear and present danger to the state.

Broadcasting is a regulated service. Broadcasters are theoretically free to do as they see fit—in fact, they operate under the shadow of a "Big Brother," the Federal Communications Commission.

To a lesser extent, broadcasters must now be concerned about the rules of the Securities and Exchange Commission, the Federal Trade Commission and the Federal Election Commission because they involve regulation of the broadcast industry.

You have probably read about the freedoms enjoyed by newspapers under the First Amendment to the Constitution. It says that Congress "shall make no law...abridging the freedom of speech, or of the press...." In theory this freedom applies also to broadcasting, but because broadcast frequencies are regulated and subject to periodic review for renewal, the practical outgrowth is that broadcasters must be more aware of potential constraints, as well as more active in fighting incursions on their First Amendment rights.

One of the gravest problems facing the broadcast industry today is the use of the FCC as a tool to threaten the broadcaster. A person or group wishing to harass a broadcaster need only write a reasonably sensible letter to the Commission to force a broadcaster into the position of having to respond in writing to defend his actions. A more sophisticated group can file various protests, or even challenge the station's license at renewal time—tying the broadcaster up in quasi-judicial proceedings for years.

The defenses are twofold—to operate in the best and most conscientious manner, complying with the Commission's rules and its implied standards; and keeping detailed, accurate files and transcripts (or transcriptions) of all material which has the potential to become involved in a legal fuss.

One of the most difficult regulatory forests which the broadcaster must traverse is called political broadcasts—it is a forest with a few tall trees and a great tangle of underbrush.

The trees being certain well-defined rules contained in the Communications Act, and the underbrush the rules and interpretations which resulted from attempts to define what the Act meant in specific instances.

Rule number one: Section 312 (a) of the Communications Act of 1934:

> (a) The Commission may revoke any station license or construction permit...
>
> (7) For willful or repeated failure to allow reasonable access to or to permit purchase of reasonable amounts of time for the use of a broadcasting station by a legally qualified candidate for Federal elective office in behalf of his candidacy.

The Section means that the congressional representatives and senators within your service area have you over a barrel!

Several educational television stations in New York State found out just how much of a barrel during the 1976 national election. Incumbent Conservative U.S. Senator James Buckley dropped a bomb on the stations by pointing out that Section 312 applied to educational, as well as commercial stations, and then demanded that the stations air a commercial film made to promote Buckley's re-election bid.

The stations reacted in various ways, with some complying promptly. Others made available free time, but demanded that Buckley agree to their format—usually an interview. At one point several of the stations simulcast a debate between Buckley and his chief competitor.

The FCC upheld Buckley. Indeed, Section 312 did make it incumbent on the stations that they permit reasonable access—but they did not have to air the commercial films as their means of complying with the regulation.

In July, 1978 the FCC tried to deal with the Buckley situation. It rules ambiguously, that noncommercial stations generally did not have to provide federal candidates lengths of program time which are not normally part of the station's schedule. However, the FCC then turned around and said that in view of the prohibition on censorship in section 315 (a) noncommercial broadcasters may not reject a candidate's material simply because it was originally prepared for broadcast on a commercial station.

A third ruling said although any station—commercial or noncommercial—may suggest a format to a candidate, the candidate is not obligated to accept it and does not lose his right to "equal opportunities" if he declines to appear on the program proposed by the station.

Stations having coverage in more than one state would be open to quite a few demands for time. Fortunately, the wording of Section 312 (a) (7) shouldn't cause any concern to commercial broadcasters, because it is hard to picture a station that wouldn't make some provision for broadcasts by legally qualified candidates for federal elective office. Any station worth its salt would not to give the public added opportunities to weight the candidates' views and qualifications.

The source of most concern and trouble for broadcasters is the famed Section 315 of the Communications Act which deals with political broadcasts. Portions of this section follow:

Section 315. (a) If any licensee shall permit any person who is a legally qualified candidate for any public office to use a broadcasting station, he shall afford equal opportunities to all other such candidates for that office in the use of such broadcasting station: *Provided*, that such licensee shall have no power of censorship over the material broadcast under the provisions of this section. No obligation is imposed under this subsection upon any licensee to allow the use of its station by any such candidates. Appearance by a legally qualified candidate on any—

1. bonda fide newscast
2. bona fide news interview
3. bona fide news documentary (if the appearance of the candidate is incidental to the presentation of the subject or subjects covered by the news documentary), or
4. on-the-spot coverage of bona fide news events (including but not limited to political conventions and activities incidental thereto.)

shall not be deemed to be use of a broadcasting station within the meaning of this subsection. Nothing in the foregoing sentence shall be construed as relieving broadcasters, in connection with the presentation of newscasts, news interviews, news documentaries and on-the-spot coverage of news events from the obligation imposed upon them under this Act to operate in the public interest and to afford reasonable opportunity for the discussion of conflicting views on issues of public importance.

Let's look more closely at the basic principles of Section 315.

First, the broadcaster has the right to make a decision whether or not to permit the use of his facilities by a legally qualified candidate. Only after the use has taken place does the section come into effect, guaranteeing all other candidates for the same office (if they are legally qualified) "equal opportunities" for the use of the station's facilities. It is extremely important that you note that the rules call for granting "equal" opportunities...not "equivalent" opportunities. This means that you do not have to provide time on, say, the same day and time of the week, as long as the time you provide is equal in amount (length) and it should be reasonably equal as to potential audience. The FCC would frown on your giving candidate A a half hour of television time at 7:30 p.m., and legally qualified candidate B, who is running for the same office, and half hour of time at midnight. (Unless Candidate B, for some reason, chose to relieve you of the burden of the obligation.)

In July, 1978 the Commission refined its definition of a "legally qualified candidate." The definition used to describe a legally qualified candidate as one who announced his candidacy and was eligible to hold the office, provided he had publically committed himself to seek election as a write-in candidate or had qualified for a place on the ballot.

The FCC now requires the candidates seeking nomination by means other than a primary election (convention or other means) must make a "substantial showing" of bona fide candidacy. The candidate, in other words, must do more than simply state he or she is running for a certain office.

Under the revisions, a person running for presidential or vice presidential nomination would not be considered a candidate until he or she had qualified for the nomination in 10 states.

With the exception of the offices of president and vice-president, no one seeking nomination to an office would be considered a legally qualified candidate more than 90 days prior to the convention or similiar procedure in which the nomination is sought.

Section 315 says you can't censor what is said by the legally qualified candidate. By the same token, the station cannot be held liable for slander committed by the candidate during the broadcast. And the prohibition against censorship DOES NOT apply to individuals who speak in behalf of a candidate, only to the candidate himself.

Second, Section 315 goes on to disencumber the news department from any obligations to the candidate, as long as the candidate's appearances come within the defined news and documentary activities. This means that if you are interviewing candidate A and candidate B comes along and demands an equal exposure, you can politely decline on principle. Of course, you may have some explaining to do if someone were to show that, over the total range of your news coverage you seemed to be giving an unbalanced presentation of one candidate's views. No good news department would have a problem with this, since balance is a basic precept of broadcast journalism. Besides, an individual who felt that your news presentation was unbalanced would have to go to considerable lengths to develop a case substantial enough to bring about interference by the FCC.

Public affairs directors should be careful about one type of programming which sometimes comes within their jurisdiction. Many stations carry reports from Congressional representatives and senators, which are sent to the station for weekly or monthly broadcasts. If that member of Congress becomes a candidate for re-election or for another office, the "Congressional Report" program becomes one under which you must grant equal opportunities to all legally qualified candidates for the same office.

The sensible solution to this dilemma is to drop this sort of program the minute the elected representative announces his or her candidacy. Then you deal with appearances of all the candidates for the specific office according to whatever policy you derive, without being forced to grant equal time because of existing programming. The Congressional member's opponents may not make a retroactive claim for equal time, based on previous airing of the program, prior to his declaration of candidacy.

Be very careful regarding incidental appearances of candidates in non-excluded programs. The mayor's incidental appearance on a morning potpourri-type program, on which the station airs news, interviews, and entertainment, might open you to a demand for equal time, if the mayor were a candidate and if the appearance was not strictly within the news and news interview exclusions.

One pitfall: If you decided to schedule a news interview program to run only around the time of or during an election compaign, the program may not be an exempt interview, simply because it cannot be demonstrated that it was a bona fide, regularly scheduled, long running—news interview program. You would have some difficulty demonstrating that the program was not created especially for the duration of the campaign period.

The solution, if you do want to do interviews related to the campaign, is to carefully schedule programs on which all the legally qualified candidates for specific offices are given an equal opportunity to appear.

This could be a debate or a news panel interview, or a call-in show, as long as you can demonstrate that the total planning and concept of the program offered equal time, and that the offer was made in writing, and that you can show what, if any, response you got from the qualified candidates. By the way, in case a candidate fails to respond, protect your interest by notifying the candidate, using registered mail or some other receipt system.

There are a number of tricky areas to be on the watch for, because they involve equal opportunity problems. If your station airs a program primarily under the control of a public official or officials, it, most likely, would not be exempt from the equal time provisions if the public official announced for office.

Thus, stations are wise to cancel "Report From The Mayor" programs, or find a non-candidate substitute during the period of candidacy.

It has probably occurred to you by now, that sometimes incumbents in office have an advantage in their access to broadcast facilities. It is true, and there is little that can be done about it, except to measure the appearance by this yardstick: "...is this a bona fide news event?"

Thus, every four years there is a healthy debate over a number of appearances by incumbent presidents, who are also candidates for nomination or re-election. Often these appearances are set in the president's role as the Chief of State, but it is obvious that the appearances have political value through simple exposure. They take advantage of the president's ability to discuss his viewpoints without fear of having to face an equal opportunity reply from competitive candidates.

The licensee must consciously make a determination that this type of appearance is a legitimate news event.

Who is a legally qualified candidate?

To define the legally qualified candidate we turn to the FCC's Rules for a definition.

> A "legally qualified candidate" means any person who has publicly announced that he is a candidate for nomination by a convention of a political party or for nomination or election in a primary, special or general election, municipal county, state or national, and who meets the qualifications prescribed by the applicable laws to hold the office for which he is a candidate so that he may be voted for by the electorate directly or by means of delegates or electors, and who:
> (1) Has qualified for a place on the ballot, or
> (2) Is eligible for a place on the ballot, or voted for by sticker, by writing in his name on the ballot, or other method, and (i) has been duly nominated by a political party which is commonly known and regarded as such, or (ii) makes a substantial showing that he is a bona fide candidate for nomination or office, as the case may be.

As you probably already suspect, there are a number of ramifications to this test.

One important concept to remember is that the candidate seeking equal opportunity must prove he is a legally qualified candidate for the office in question.

You should be aware that the person must be a candidate for a "public office," thus eliminating some categories of elective offices, such as delegates to a party convention.

The one big problem is that, as the FCC rules show, a person does not have to have his or her name printed on the ballot to be a "legally qualified candidate"—if that person can prove that he or she is making a *bona fide* run for office. This aspect applies particularly in situations where write-in candidates are permitted. But it does not mean that just because you can write a person's name in on the ballot, that the person is a "legally qualified candidate." The candidate has to demonstrate bona fide candidacy. Even if the person makes a public announcement of candidacy, the FCC permits stations to establish rules to require reasonable proof of the bona fide nature of the candidacy.

But remember that public announcement, especially in the case of minor offices can consist of going down to the election board and filing papers signifying that one is a candidate for an office. In some states candidates get their names on the ballot by filing petitions signed by a small percentage of the appropriate group of voters.

Also, there is a difference between appearing to be a candidate and publically announcing candidacy. Thus some potential candidates conduct a number of activities which draw themselves into the public light when they are preparing to run, but they do not in the eyes of the FCC become legally qualified candidates, until they announce their candidacy.

Persons may be eliminated as "legally qualified candidates" by ruling of the courts or, in the absence of a judicial ruling, by appropriate officials, such a state attorney general.

Notice that FCC rules go into considerable depth in describing the types of elections which are covered, including primary and general elections, as well as special elections at the municipal, county, state and federal levels. The rules also point out that elections in which the voters choose electors, who cast the final votes are covered by the equal opportunity provision. This, of course, applies to the presidential election.

One final thought, when dealing with legally qualified candidates, you may treat the groups of candidates for nomination from different parties separately. You must treat all candidates for one office within one party equally, but not necessarily as you would treat those of another party. Put simply, you could, in theory, afford equal opportunities to Democratic candidates for mayor, while excluding all Republican candidates for mayor in the primary election.

EQUAL OPPORTUNITIES

The matter of providing equal opportunities becomes very complicated for station managers, who must consider both free and paid appearances by legally qualified candidates.

However, for public affairs and editorial directors the problems are a little less complicated, since they do not have to be concerned with paid advertisements.

To start with, if you are farsighted enough to set aside time for free political appearances, and you set out to create an equal opportunity situation, you will eliminate most valid claims against your station. It takes a great deal of organization and considerable followup, but thorough planning can save a lot of last minute agony as election day draws near.

Most stations have defined policies to deal with candidates who refuse to appear live. Those who refuse to appear at all are clearly identified, so that there can be no misunderstanding and no later claim for time. Candidates who send in prepared materials are another problem. Under Section 315—as interpreted by the FCC—a station does not have the right to demand only live appearances of candidates. Thus, if you have an equal opportunity situation, you must accept transcribed materials. Most stations will air the material, if it reasonably fits into the stated format for the program. Usually the station will make clear, in announcements before and after, that the candidate's appearance was taped and supplied to the station, and that the candidate had chosen not to appear in person. This is to make clear why the candidate did not participate in the give and take of the program, if it were a debate or interview format.

One significant problem is to find enough time to accommodate all the legally qualified candidates. One factor is the number of offices which the station opens to candidate appearances. Most stations plan some sort of public affairs format to accommodate congressional candidates, major statewide candidates, and major county and municipal candidates. Frequently, minor offices in the state, county and municipal categories are not included. Typically, time is made available for candidates for Congress, governor and lieutenant governor, membership on the county commission, mayor, and membership on the city council or board of aldermen.

As you can easily visualize, we already have a potential for a fair number of candidates making appearances. In a general election you automatically have at least two candidates for most offices (Democratic and Republican), and you may have other parties on the ballot. The other factor is the number of individual seats to be filled in your coverage area. You could easily have two congressional districts—which would mean four possible candidates. Even if there were only one municipality in your area, you might have upwards of five seats to fill on the board of aldermen or the council.

Jim Hart, who was general manager of WXII-TV in Winston-Salem, North Carolina, says that during one election his station had 97 candidates appear on its programs in one primary election alone.

When talking about equal opportunities remember it does not mean equal time, nor precisely the same day and time for an appearance. However, there cannot be gross discrepancies between the time of an appearance by one candidate and the time of an appearance by another.

Another interesting point. A station is not obliged to notify a candidate that free time has been given to his opposition, but wise public affairs directors avoid this issue by making provisions for appearances by all legally qualified candidates for any office for which appearances are planned. You must remember that you are operating under the Fairness Doctrine as well. The Doctrine mandates positive outreach to include all sides of community controversies.

Once you have set up a program opportunity for all candidates for one office, you may require them to waive their rights to other equal opportunities, if they are either unable or unwilling to appear. If a candidate refuses to agree to such a waiver, you are left with a difficult choice—provide that candidate with time, if requested, on some other occasion, or cancel the program.

Another example of the problems you must deal with in planning political broadcast time: In some states a single candidate may appear on the ballot under more than one party label. For instance, in New York State it isn't unusual for a Republican or Democratic candidate to be endorsed, separately, by the main party and what amounts to a Liberal or Conservative wing, under another party label and organization. Thus, the candidate's name appears on two separate rows on the ballot, and many voters mark off the candidate according to the party label they prefer.

For our purposes, these party labels mean nothing. You give equal opportunity to *the candidate* not the party. So you may rightfully reject or compress multiple appearances by the same candidate, even if he is endorsed by more than one party.

Station managers, program and public affairs directors have to be on the alert for national, so-called non-exempt programs which they carry, on which candidates in their service area appear. For instance, if a senator from your coverage area were running for re-election, and for some reason or another appeared in a non-news role on a network program, you would have to afford an equal opportunity to the senator's opponents.

THE CAMPAIGN COMMUNICATIONS REFORM ACT OF 1971

The Campaign Communications Reform Act of 1971 was passed in order to add a new section to Section 312 of the Communications Act. The new section says:

> A station license may be revoked: "for willful or repeated failure to allow reasonable access to or to permit purchase of reasonable amounts of time for the use of a broadcasting station by a legally qualified candidate for federal elective office on behalf of his candidacy."

In the literature of FCC rules the term "reasonable access" has come to be used to describe this section.

In its July 1978 amendments the FCC said reasonable access for federal candidates must be provided at least during the 45 days prior to a primary and the 60 days before a general election.

Primarily this section is intended to make certain that candidates for federal elective office may buy political advertising time. But the new provision does indicate that a station could reasonably be expected to carry some broadcasts on which candidates appear.

> The FCC stated in its Guideline VIII, 3 that: "Each licensee, under the provisions of Section 307 and 309 of the Communications Act, is required to serve the public interest, convenience or necessity. In its Report and Statement of Policy Re: Commission En Banc Programming Inquiry (1960), the Commission stated that political broadcasts constitute one of the major elements in meeting that standard.... The foregoing broad standard has been applied over the years to the overall programming of licensees. New Section 312 (a) (7))(reasonable access) adds to that broad standard specific language concerning reasonable access."

While the reasonable access provision doesn't specifically require stations to give free time to legally qualified federal candidates, the real impact is—yes, you must provide reasonable access to legally qualified candidates for federal office.

The FCC and the Communications Act do not demand reasonable access for state and local offices, but a station is required to make a "good-faith judgment if it decides," to eliminate an office from its political broadcast plans.

What Congress and the Commission have been trying to do is give broadcasters a message: Appearances by political candidates can be expected, reasonably, to be part of your programming, although you may make good-faith judgments on just what non-federal offices you include.

Another impact of the rules, regulations and interpretations is to say—don't get caught denying access to a political candidate for reasons which you cannot defend. In very blunt terms, you better not be caught shutting off access to people you personally dislike, parties you do not wish to support or to minorities.

When all the dust has settled, the intent of the various rules is sensible, and can be met by any station providing its management takes the time to logically plot out guidelines well ahead of each political season.

The simplest way is to say, we're going to allow a certain amount of time for free appearances by candidates for office within programs we control. Then decide the time allocations, the offices to be covered, tell all the eligibles what you are doing, and set about getting their commitments to appear.

There is still the whole area of paid political advertising, which is outside the responsibility of a public affairs director. After you've spent several hours wrestling with the logistics of putting on a series of political appearances, just breathe a sigh of relief that you are not responsible for advertising!

The best defense against regulation is a good offense. Plan your station's public affairs activities to include ample and equal opportunities for political candidates, and you'll be all set.

Time Limits

The FCC says that a candidate wishing to make a claim under the equal opportunities concept must make that request within one week (7 days) of the prior use which gave rise to the claim. If the claimant had not yet filed for office when the prior use occurred, the claim would be valid only if filed within one week of the first subsequent use after the claimant became a candidate.

This leads to one complication. If your station is airing a regularly scheduled report to the people by an official who is an unopposed candidate, and suddenly opposition appears, you must either give equal opportunities, if requested, or cancel the program. This is why most stations establish a terminal date for all programs of this nature, if the elected representative is up for re-nomination or re-election, even if unopposed.

Limitations on a Candidate

Section 315 of the Communications Act specifically prohibits the censorship of any broadcast by a legally qualified candidate. Thus, even though the script may contain libelous material, you must permit its broadcast. Fortunately, the U.S. Supreme Court has held stations blameless in civil suits due to the specific demands of Section 315.

There can be no excuse for censorship under this section. One popular example—what if the candidate's statement contains remarks which might be inflamatory or offensive in the community. The answer is the same—you cannot censor!

But—and this is a big but—the no censorship rule applies to the candidate, and the candidate alone. A station may freely censor the script or content of a program presented by someone in behalf of a candidate.

The no censorship rule is so absolute that a station cannot prevent (although it should be on record as advising against) the broadcast of obscene or defamatory material. Of course, the candidate who broadcasts obscene material might be interested in the text of Paragraph 1464, Appendix C. Title 18. of the United States Criminal Code:

> "Whoever utters any obscene, indecent or profane language by means of radio communication shall be fined not more than $10,000 or imprisoned not more than two years, or both." (June 25, 1948. Ch. 645. 62 Stat. 769).

The FCC, at this writing, is studying possible revisions of this section of Title 18.

The FCC has made it clear that under Section 315 the candidate may use the allotted time in any manner desired, and may not be required to provide an advance text of the script, although this is often done informally to assist the station in the production of the program or spot announcement.

THE FAIRNESS DOCTRINE AND POLITICAL BROADCASTS

To restate the principle of the Fairness Doctrine: A station must permit reasonable opportunity for the presentation of views which contrast those of persons who originally presented a controversial issue of public importance.

The Doctrine deals with issues—not candidates. This makes the job of the station management more difficult, because someone must constantly monitor issues affecting the community, and make certain that the station gives ample opportunities for full discussion of these issues.

The obligation falls on the station in the case of an enquiry by the FCC. The station must show that it has acted reasonably and in good faith in meeting its obligations.

The Commission has suggested that one way to define a "controversial issue of public importance" is to make "a subjective evaluation of the impact that the issue is likely to have on the community at large."

The Commission has indicated that one way to do this is to measure "the degree of attention paid an issue by government officials, community leaders, and the media." If the issue is one on which the community will vote—such as a bond referendum—it would be pretty apparent that the referendum is a community issue.

Remember that when dealing with controversial issues, they may be national, regional or local in nature, and if one aspect of any such issue is covered, then other major aspects must be covered.

Under the Fairness Doctrine, the station can demonstrate compliance through a number of means, such as showing news coverage, discussions on interview or round-table programs or coverage within a documentary.

There is no call for equal time, other than a showing of reasonableness and lack of strong bias towards the presentation of one or another viewpoint in preference to contrasting viewpoints.

The ascertainment procedure set forth by the FCC calls on the licensee to identify major viewpoints and shades of opinion. There is no obligation to cover all issues or all viewpoints, but the licensee should be aware of the shades of opinion and be prepared to explain why some were excluded, if that be the case.

The Fairness Doctrine applies to political broadcasts only in that you should make ample provision to discuss important issues in relation to the political campaign. This is another reason for inviting candidates to appear on station-controlled programs. You can consult your ascertainment files, define some important issues and viewpoints held in the area covered by the political offices and pose these questions to the candidates.

Your resources may provide excellent ammunition for the news department in thinking about questions to be asked during interviews with political candidates. This is one solid reason for committing the issues discovered in the ascertainment process to paper, and circulating these findings among staff members at frequent intervals.

One area which requires care from public affairs directors. If there are referendum times on your local ballots, you should be careful to see that they get full and ample discussion and coverage. This might apply to a statewide referendum on pollution control, referendum on bonds to finance highways or a local vote on annexation.

The FCC has left the choice of who should represent a viewpoint to the licensee. There are those who would like to see some type of system of mandated access. The best defense against this line of thought is a good offense. The station should actively seek to air the many views of its community, being sure to include even the most outspoken exponents of viewpoints as well as the more moderate spokepersons.

The Fairness Doctrine is under continuous assault, and it is only through vigorous participation by broadcasters that the industry is going to keep the doctrine from becoming a device for bureaucratic dictation of what voices shall be heard on stations. This is not the purpose of our free press, and it is up to the broadcasters themselves to defend their rightful freedom under the First Amendment by (1) doing a good conscientious job and (2) fighting in the courts every time someone tries to unlawfully modify this right.

THE "ZAPPLE" DOCTRINE

In a 1970 letter to Nicholas Zapple, the FCC extablished what is known as the quasi-equal opportunities or "Zapple Doctrine." It says that when a station sells time to supporters or spokespersons for a candidate—during an election campaign—the licensee must afford comparable time to spokespersons for the opponent. Typically, the people taking advantage of quasi-equal opportunities might be discussing the campaign issue, urging the election of their candidate or criticizing the opponent.

There are two aspects of this doctrine of interest to public affairs directors. First, if candidate one's supporters bought their time, you do not have to provide a second candidate's supporters with free time. But, if a station grants free time to the supporters of candidate one, then it must grant free time to supporters of candidate two.

If the candidate appears on your program, you go by the equal opportunity requirements of Section 315 and not the Zapple Doctrine.

The newscast exemptions of Section 315 continue to apply to supporters of a candidate, just as they do the candidate. Thus you can interview a movie star who is stumping for a favorite candidate, as long as you're engaged in legitimate news coverage.

Another interesting aspect of the quasi-equal opportunities doctrine—it does not have to apply equally to all candidates. A station may pass judgment on the relative importance of a candidate and thus—on its judgment that the candidate is not a significant factor in the election—decline to give his supporters quasi-equal opportunity time.

THE PERSONAL ATTACK RULES

The FCC promulgated a set of rules relating to personal attacks on August 14, 1967.

A personal attack is defined as an attack on the *honesty, character, integrity or personal qualities of an identified person or group*. However, the statements must be in reality an *attack*, not just a passing mention or reference.

The personal attack rule reads as follows:

(a) When, during the presentation of views on a controversial issue of public importance, an attack is made upon the honesty, character, integrity or like personal qualifications of an identified person or group, the licensee shall, within a reasonable time and in no event later than 1 week after the attack, transmit to the person or group attacked (1) notification of the date, time and identification of the broadcast; (2) a script or tape (or an accurate summary if a script or tape is not available) of the attack; and (3) an offer of a reasonable opportunity to respond over the licensee's facilities.

(b) The provisions of paragraph (a) of this section shall not be applicable (i) to attacks on foreign groups or foreign public figures; (ii) to personal attacks which are made by legally qualified candidates, their authorized spokesmen, or those associated with them in the campaign; and (iii) to *bona fide* newscasts, *bona fide* news interviews, and on-the-spot coverage of a *bona fide* news event (including commentary or analysis contained in the foregoing programs, but the provisions of paragraph (2) shall be applicable to editorials of the licensee).

Note: The Fairness Doctrine is applicable to situations coming within (iii), above, and, in a specific factual situation, may be applicable in the general area of political broadcasts (ii), above.

This chapter is devoted to political broadcasts, and, in the context of political broadcasts, note that the personal attack rule generally does not apply. There is one trap. If a legally qualified candidate were to attack a non-candidate, non-spokesperson, then the station would be required to make the personal attack notification, even though the Communications Act forbids censoring the candidate's statement containing the personal attack.

Now, a flip of the coin. If a non-candidate attacks a candidate, the station may require that the reply be made by someone other than the candidate to avoid getting into a Section 315 equal opportunity situation.

Of concern to a public affairs director is the fact that the personal attack rule applies to editorials and news documentaries.

Many stations take the time to have their legal counsel define which programs on the schedule have potential for personal attack problems, and a regular system of monitoring is set up, so that if a broadcast contains an apparent personal attack it can be ruled on by counsel and the legal notification made.

For many stations, the problem may be minimal if the schedule contains few programs with potential for this sort of programming approach. Editorials, of course, are easy to police, and besides, the station should have a regular editorial distribution and notification system to comply with the fairness doctrine.

One editorial director, Peter Kohler of WCBS-TV, New York, said he ran across only one or two of his editorials in a year which would be subject to the personal attack rule—but Kohler said he also sees no reason why a station should not launch an occasional personal attack in an editorial, and welcome the reply of the person or group attacked. It acts as a stimulus to free and open discussion of controversial issues of public importance.

A station which airs a large amount of commercial and non-commercial political programming is very careful about its internal procedures as election day approaches.

This station bans any political news stories involving charges by the candidates against their opponents on the Sunday and Monday before election Tuesday, and on election Tuesday itself. Appearances by candidates are banned on any programs over the same period.

The station also sends out a form letter to all candidates setting forth its policies for the final days of the campaign. What follows is a portion of that letter:

"As recommended by the Fair Campaign Practices Committee, we have again adopted the following policy to prevent unfair *last minute* attacks during the closing days of this campaign.

XXXX news reporters will accept releases and statements from you and your opponent only until midnight of the Thursday before Election Day. This information may be broadcast during the day on Friday.

XXXX will not broadcast any last minute charges brought by your opponent—or vice versa—after our last broadcast at midnight, Friday.

However, should any issue develop in the final days, we will be available to make a determination on its urgency and pertinence. But obviously we'll be extremely skeptical of any issue which has not emerged prior to the closing days of the campaign. In the event of a last minute issue, we will discuss and investigate it thoroughly. We are asking, again this year, that the chairman of the four parties be available as they have been in the past to give us a bi-partisan judgment on the validity of any charges made in the final days.

Special Note: Comments of a political nature will not be allowed on...*Open Line*, effective Saturday."

EDITORIAL ENDORSEMENTS

Editorializing by broadcast stations is becoming more common. However, taking stands on political personalities and issues is far less common. It takes quite a bit of courage to endorse a specific candidate or take a stand on one side or another of a referendum issue. On the other hand, some stations report that their vigorous stands on personalities and issues have drawn just the sort of public attention they have desired, enhancing their image as leaders in the community.

The most important thing to remember about a political editorial is to be certain to get a copy of the editorial into the hands of the opposition candidate or candidates promptly, and to be safe, secure a receipt indicating delivery of the transcript. If the opposition candidates request an opportunity to reply after receiving your transcript and invitation, you will move promptly to comply with their wishes.

The FCC has promulgated specific rules (effective August 14, 1967) which affect political editorials, and they follow:

> (c) Where a licensee, in an editorial, (i) endorses or (ii) opposes a legally qualified candidate or candidates, the licensee shall, within 24 hours after the editorial, transmit to respectively (i) the other qualified candidate or candidates for the same office or (ii) the candidate opposed in the editorial (1) notification of the date and time of the editorial; (2) a script or tape of the editorial; and (3) an offer of a reasonable opportunity for a candidate or spokesman of the candidate to respond over the licensee's facilities; *Provided, however,* that where such editorials are broadcast within 72 hours prior to the day of the election, the licensee shall comply with the provisions of this paragraph sufficiently far in advance of the broadcast to enable the candidate or candidates to have a reasonable opportunity to prepare a response and to present it in a timely fashion.

In permitting a reply by the opposition, a station may reasonably limit replies to spokespersons for candidates to avoid the obligations of Section 315, which would call for appearances by other candidates in what could become an unending cycle.

One quicksand trap: Do NOT introduce a reply under the political editorial rule by stating that the station has endorsed another candidate. This, in itself, acts as a further endorsement and opens up new time requirements.

If you decide to take a stand on an issue under discussion in a current political campaign, be aware that if you specifically praise or criticize a candidate, you fall under the political editorializing rule.

The most practical approach is to deal with the issue, not personalities, in a case like this.

The political editorializing rules do not apply to editorials which deal with ballot items—say a referendum or authorization of a bond issue. In this case, you would only have to show that somewhere in the station's public affairs programming and news coverage, there had been adequate coverage of all sides to the ballot item controversy.

NEWS COVERAGE

The amended version of the Communications Act frees the content of a bona fide newscast, news interview, news documentary or on-the-spot coverage of a bona fide news event from specific equal opportunity requirements.

The Fairness Doctrine applies to the overall fairness of a station's coverage of controversial issues of public importance, but does not specifically require either equal opportunities or fairness within a newscast or within the station's news coverage. Requirements of the Fairness Doctrine are met through a station's total programming.

What is important in the news area is a good sound journalistic principle—every action has a reaction—and you are not doing your job if you fail to seek out reaction on important issues, or if you ignore the many facets of a controversy.

Herein you answer not to the FCC, but to the professional standards of journalism and the need for free discussion in a democracy.

There is one aspect of Section 315 which has been of great interest to news directors and their public affairs counterparts.

It is the controversy over debates by major candidates. You may recall that in the 1960 national election the networks persuaded Congress to lift, temporarily, the provisions of Section 315 setting forth equal time (now called equal opportunity) requirements for candidates for public office. The networks wanted to broadcast live debates between John F. Kennedy and Richard M. Nixon without having to make time available to the minority candidates, who clearly did not play a significant factor in the presidential election. There were a total of four debates in 1960 under the suspension of Section 315.

After what was regarded as a successful test of the idea, the suspension was allowed to lapse, and since then the networks have been unsuccessful in their drive to get a permanent suspension of Section 315 to permit presidential debates.

In the fall of 1975, the FCC made an interpretation of the equal time rule which permits broadcasters to cover debates between major party candidates without having to grant equal time, providing the debate itself is held outside the broadcast studios and is arranged by an outside group.

In the 1976 presidential election the two candidates President Gerald Ford and Democratic nominee Jimmy Carter agreed to a series of "debates" which were to be held in various cities under the auspices of the League of Women Voters. The format called for questions to be posed by a panel of reporters. There were disputes over the composition of the panels.

Another fight broke out over League ground rules for the televising of the debates. The League didn't want the networks to take camera shots of the audience to show reaction, while the networks contended that it was a violation of their First Amendment rights to be told how to cover a story.

The League held to its rules and the debates—three for the presidential nominees and one for the vice presidential nominees—took place.

While the Section 315 matter remains unresolved in the minds of the networks, it is clear that the 1976 election year experiment lessened the chances for Amendment of the Communications Act.

CREATIVE USE OF PUBLIC AFFAIRS TIME TO COVER POLITICAL ISSUES

Creativity is partly the expenditure of personal energy. Creativity stems from doing something yourself—thinking, working, producing—rather than copying or letting the other fellow lead you. Partly, it is doing the new, the different, the original.

Creativity in the public affairs area consists first in thinking out and analyzing your community's needs and the station's resources, and then acting to provide the best and most responsive programming you can within these resources.

Creativity is lifting your programming out of the humdrum onto a level where it becomes stimulating—interesting—to your audience.

Many, many stations work hard to devise a satisfactory balance of opportunities to schedule political appearances, so that the audience can have a chance to hear and see the candidates to get some idea of their respective stands on important issues.

But the falling down point is in the execution of the program. It is far more difficult to make a program interesting, than it is to simply provide the program.

One way to improve any program is to provide a stimulating interplay among the participants. There is nothing worse than inviting two or three competitors for an office and having an unqualified station spokesperson interview them. The interviewer, if there is one, should be the best available person, someone who is familiar with the issues, the candidates and the community.

It's probably better to limit the appearances by the candidates to one person at a time, and have a small panel doing the questioning. That way you have more time to question one individual, and more

Fig. 7-1. Covering an election at WVOX, New Rochelle, New York. Left to right, Peter Allen of WVOX, Ogden Reid, guest commentator, former ambassador and congressman; and Edwin G. Michaelian, director of Pace University Institute for Sub-Urban Governance and former Westchester Country Executive. (Photo courtesy of WVOX).

diversity of questions. Select a varied panel, and if your staff needs beefing up, look for outside panelists. They might come from the nearby wire service bureau, a newspaper, or perhaps a university political science department. (It's always good to have a couple of academic persons on whom you can rely when you need help with political analysis.) (Fig. 7-1)

When constructing a panel, try for diverse individuals. If you have a political reporter, then, of course, he or she should be included. If minority issues are important to the campaign, try to include someone who knows minority problems. If one reporter is rough and bores in on questions, select another who appears to be smooth and easygoing. You should set out to give your guest a thorough grilling—that is why you are doing the program, and your guest would be naive to accept an invitation thinking you would do otherwise.

In dealing with issues, consider other ways to illustrate your points. Instead of programming a dull studio panel, a radio station could go out and do man-on-the-street interviews, or other on-scene taping to emphasize some aspects of the issues; and then have a studio discussion of various aspects. For instance, your state is planning a highway bond issue. Talk to truckers at truck stops, talk to highway patrol officers, interview some motorists and talk to representatives of the auto club.

Then you have the option of doing a documentary style broadcast, in which various viewpoints are expressed by the interviewees through intercutting and narration to tie them together. Or you can play excerpts of these tapes and ask for comments from the candidates themselves. You can even add to the interplay by having your listening audience call in to comment.

For television, the same techniques hold—only you have the advantage of being able to visualize problems. This means that even with a low budget, you can shoot tape or film to illustrate some of the points of the highway controversy, even if you don't have the manpower to do extensive interviewing. A well-planned half day of shooting by a photographer or tape cameraperson would be enough time to provide ample visuals to back up a studio presentation.

One major fault of public affairs programming is that it tends to be dull and listless. This is mainly because many stations do not give their public affairs staff a mandate to make their programming fully as good as the news or entertainment programs. The mandate has to be backed up with personnel and facilities. On the other hand there are a handful of stations which do a superb production job on their public affairs programs and, in some cases, can report healthy audiences for their efforts.

Chapter 8
Public Information:
Commercial and
Non-Profit Organizations

This chapter looks at public affairs programming primarily from the viewpoint of the people who approach broadcast stations seeking public affairs exposure, and from the viewpoint of those in broadcasting who must use the services of public relations representatives.

Our purpose is to offer some assistance to those who speak for outside organizations, and some insight to those who bear the public affairs responsibility at broadcast stations.

The job titles may differ: public relations director, public affairs manager, publicity committee chairperson, or communications director. But the mission is the same—tell an organization's story through the use of free exposure on public affairs programs.

Almost all business organizations of any size have some sort of public relations structure. It may be one person or a huge department, broken into specialists in such areas as employee communications, public relations, community relations and stockholder relations.

Most private non-profit organizations have entered the public relations field.

The term public relations has gotten a bad reputation. Most of the blame must fall on practitioners who have failed to realize that the public affairs time set aside by broadcast stations is not reserved for the promotion of ventures for commercial gain. Too often in the past, individuals engaged in pure publicity or promotional functions have called themselves public relations representatives. They have barged into stations peddling their wares without knowing, or caring to know, anything about the public affairs obligations, purposes, or capabilities of the stations.

We can say from experience that the people who practice the skill of public relations today are well aware of those who may have besmirched their reputation, and there is a great move afoot to professionalize the public relations field.

In addition, a great many competent people have entered the public relations profession, and they are training newcomers in the many skills needed to effectively carry out their duties.

Generally speaking, broadcast station public affairs directors encounter more public relations representatives from non-profit organizations than from commercial companies. The non-profit organizations have a far greater need of free exposure and fewer opportunities to gain public attention. They also deal in matters which are more closely attuned to community needs such as health, children, social problems and education.

Today, approaches are frequently made by book publishers who wish to have authors interviewed. This can be a very healthy relationship. Most networks and stations will consider authors of non-fiction works, if their areas of expertise match discerned areas of audience interest.

For example, during the energy crisis of the early 1970s a number of very informative non-fiction books were published for popular consumption. Their authors received wide attention because public affairs and news directors across the country were anxious to locate and talk with people who had a understanding and overview of the energy crisis. They were usually chosen because they were not partisans of the public power, petrochemical, or conservation factions.

Each year a number of general books are published on topics such as education, religion and medicine. Their authors frequently receive wide attention from broadcasters.

This is an example of a commercial organization making an approach to the media in which a legitimate purpose is served, even though the commercial organization (the publisher) may eventually benefit through the sale of its product.

We should note that most interviews of this sort de-emphasize the book, and what actually happens is that the author's recognition factor is raised. This means that, later on, if you wander into a book store, you may recall the author's name on a book on display.

Some commercial organizations make it a standard practice to have available experts, who will appear on interview programs and participate in documentary programs.

For example: The utility industry and the petrochemical industry have both been targets of criticism by conservationists and people concerned about nuclear waste and accidents. As a result many companies within these fields have actively worked to let broadcasters know that anytime they want to interview an expert representing their side of the controversy, one will be made available—often a top executive of the firm.

This fits right into the concept of the Fairness Doctrine, because if you're going to interview an opponent of nuclear power plants, you certainly have an obligation to interview someone who speaks for the nuclear power industry.

There will always be some individuals who will try to get you to do a feature on the circus or a new vegetable slicer. Sometimes there is a time and place for this sort of thing, but most stations find few times and fewer places for such outright promotional or commercial ventures. There are just so many other worthy ideas wandering around.

Many so-called non-profit organizations represent profitmaking groups or individuals. For example, the American Bar Association and the American Medical Association are non-profit organizations, but they represent profit-making organizations and individuals.

By virtue of their functions as coordinating and research organizations, these groups make excellent literature available to the general public and point out fluent interviewees on topics of general concern. They are particularly good if you wish to gather research materials, such as reports on health issues; or wish to determine the official stand of a large professional organization; or need to pinpoint an individual who has just the expertise you are seeking for a documentary or public affairs interview.

A call to Chicago and the AMA may locate a doctor a few blocks from your studios who is an outstanding expert on medical malpractice issues. Ironically, this sort of fact may not surface in your daily contacts within the community.

These organizations are also helpful because they know what's going on at regional medical centers, and in their state and county affiliates. They often know when an outstanding person in their speciality is going to be in your region, and can help you to set up an interview.

Other non-profit organizations represent churches, charities, research projects and social issue groups. These are, in a sense, the purest of the pure, since often all they have to "sell" are ideas—a wider discussion of political or social issues.

If you were working on a documentary of kidney disease, a call to the National Kidney Foundation—which collects funds to support research on kidney diseases—will result in a wealth of information. The Foundation can pinpoint institutions and individuals in your area who can be contacted for interviews. The author once used this resource and not only obtained access to some of the top kidney transplant specialists in the country, but was able to interview a number of kidney dialysis and transplant patients.

If you are working on a political issue, contact the League of Women Voters. They take fierce pride in their non-partisan analysis of political and social issues.

Our point is professional public relations people can also be of tremendous help to public affairs directors because they know what you need, and how to pinpoint the information and people who will be most helpful.

Experienced news and public affairs people establish solid contacts with reliable public relations representatives. While you frequently want to reach a top organization or company official, you may be most effective if you go through a trusted public relations representative—one who will be an advocate of your cause.

A good public relations person can save many hours when you're doing research or looking for experts. Say you're doing an editorial attacking the trucking industry. If you have good contacts among trucking firms and industry organizations, you can quickly and easily locate someone to do an editorial reply. This is the simple and efficient way to see that you fulfill your Fairness Doctrine obligations.

Another example in which a good file of public relations contacts comes in handy: The government acts to regulate the use of certain compounds in agricultural weed killers. If you're in a farming area, you may want to put your finger on appropriate farm and industry spokespersons. A handful of calls to good PR contacts should help you locate them.

All of which points out that there can be healthy and creative relationship between the staff of the broadcast station and PR practitioners.

BROADCAST STATIONS—FROM A PR PERSON'S VIEW

Former broadcaster and present-day packager of programs about the New York City School System, Murray Roberts, has this advice for public relations people:

Roberts says: "You have to judge the needs of the people that you're going to. If you go to a radio station or a TV station just saying 'hey, this is what I need," forget it, you are not going to get it. You have to really figure out what they need, and why they should be using you, and how it fits in with what you're doing."

What Roberts is saying holds true for almost any venture in which you deal with other people. If you are a sales representative, you have to get to know the needs of your potential customers. If you are a minister, you need to know the problems of your parishioners. If you are a teacher, you must know your pupils' homes and community.

If you are doing public relations work, you need to know how broadcasters operate and how their personnel think.

If you don't already have practical experience in the field, study your broadcasting contacts. Visit stations, tour their facilities, have lunch with executives and staff members, take courses, become familiar with operational techniques, read the trade publications, study FCC rules and National Association of Broadcasters' policies.

Many public relations people come out of print media backgrounds. They have gained a solid understanding of journalistic techniques, but there are important differences between the way broadcast stations operate and the way newspapers function.

One basic difference. The newspaper is primarily a medium for the transmission of news. Broadcast stations are primarily transmitters of entertainment. Therefore, their news and public affairs activities take up only a limited portion of their total air time, personnel and budget. The difference is that broadcast stations are frequently unable to respond to requests for news or public affairs coverage with the same staff as a newspaper.

Newspapers are subject only to limited regulation. If a newspaper publisher wishes to accept articles promoting products or services, it is his privilege. Broadcasters have a strong community service mandate, which makes them far less willing to use public affairs time for the promotion of purely commercial ventures.

Chapters 5, 6 and 7 of this book dealt with the regulatory framework surrounding broadcasting. Public relations representatives need to be aware of these constraints, because of the way they influence the people whom PR agents deal with at stations.

As in any venture which involves selling—whether you're selling ideas or merchandise—find out whom to contact.

Whom you contact depends upon the size of the organization. At a small radio station, you might start with the general manager, since he or she will play an important part in any activity of the station. At a slightly larger radio station your contact will be the program director or the news director, depending on how their duties are split up.

Television stations and major market radio stations can afford larger staffs, and it is not unusual to have someone designated to oversee public affairs programming and another person designated to oversee editorials.

In this case, your contacts may include the news director for hard news, the public affairs director for interviews, and the editorial director, in case you wish to respond to an editorial or provide some data.

At very large television stations and at the networks, public relations representatives have to find out who produces what shows, and become acquainted with the specific producers, since they make decisions about who is interviewed and what subjects are covered.

In general, an initial contact should be preceded by a telephone call to set up a brief get acquainted meeting. This should be devoted to making sure that the station person has the necessary information about whom to contact (day and night) at your organization. You might leave some background information for file purposes, including, if you have them available, some color slides for TV stations.

The other objective of this type of meeting is to find out quickly the types of programs aired by the station on which you might be helpful. There may be certain interview programs or documentary projects, with which the station will seek your advice or help.

The author has found a wide diversity of opinion on lunch dates with public relations representatives. It seems generally that key broadcast executives in the news and public affairs area tend to be very busy, and thus limit their luncheon dates—often finding that they have too many obligatory civic luncheons to attend anyway.

There are some individuals who will let you buy them lunch anytime, and you might wonder, justifiably, how busy and how important these individuals are.

Producers often have wide fluctuations in their work load and are amenable to luncheon meetings with key contacts when time is available. These sessions can be highly productive.

The author recalls a public relations representative who would insist quite frequently that they should have lunch sometime. The author and the PR person finally met one day at a professional meeting, and in ten minutes exchanged the information they needed to swap!

A wise public relations person makes occasional brief visits to key station contacts, just to make certain that they are still aware of his or her existence, and to keep tabs on changes in personnel.

You should develop a file by station with lists of programs and related information, such as format, host and producer. You are interested in programs on which you might place guests or provide information which could be credited to your organization.

Bill Glance headed the Office of Information at the Bowman Gray School of Medicine at Wake Forest University in North Carolina. Glance gives a good example of how close dealings with a local television station's public affairs director yielded many beneficial exposures for his medical center.

Glance said he and the station's public affairs director discussed possible public affairs programming. That discussion, said Glance, led to the development of a series of interviews on medical and health topics. These interviews were telecast live every other Friday on the station's "Midmorning Show."

Glance said: "I organize the topics and arrange for members of the faculty and staff of the Bowman Gray School of Medicine and North Carolina Baptist Hospital to be available to be interviewed."

The series has covered such diverse areas, said Glance, as "childhood cancer, noise pollution, recreational therapy, ultrasound, kidney transplantation, epilepsy, cardiovascular research on monkeys, sports medicine and many, many more."

This seems to be an extraordinary amount of air time for one organization, except that it happens to be the only teaching center in the area and the only other medical center—a county hospital—has frequently employed less skilled advocates of its cause. Hence, the county facility hasn't fared as well in telling its story.

Brush Moser worked in broadcast communications for the United Methodist Church. His organization has long and well established contacts with the national media, but must frequently make publicity plans for short-term situations in major cities around the country—such as a major meeting of the church hierarchy. Moser says he seeks advice from knowledgeable local sources, including the local and state Council of Churches offices and then he prepares material specifically for local broadcast stations.

Moser said: "I prepare a sheet listing the guests (those he proposes are among those attending the meeting), according to the issues which I feel would be of most interest to the producer."

Moser says he tries to learn as much as he can about stations and programs which might want to interview his guests. "What I prefer to do is to get well enough acquainted with the program to be able to offer a guest who fits into the atmosphere, mood, theme, or image of the show. In other words, one who is *simpatico*...some programs feature show biz personalities, others are more issue oriented, while others try to keep their audiences (women, men, etc.) in mind. We try to offer a resource person who has expertise, charisma and the gift of gab. We don't offer persons who we have not seen 'perform' or who have not been recommended by trusted colleagues."

If you have an idea for a program or news feature, go out and sell it. Leonard Tropin, is vice-president of the National Council on

Crime and Delinquency, said: "The best way to get on the air...has been to approach a producer or newscaster with an idea. Although we routinely send out releases on policy statements and other news, we do not place much hope in their amounting to anything."

Tropin also points out that his organization is a resource for information regarding crime and delinquency. "Over the years this agency has supplied information, statistics, opinions and other assistance to...news people and especially those making documentaries in our field. So we have established contacts who know us well enough to listen to an idea. That is the most profitable way of obtaining TV coverage."

The author recalls a situation in which a major documentary unit was launching into a series on justice. He prevailed on Tropin to run a highly concentrated seminar on issues for the producers of the series, which brought them up to date and broadened their perspectives on the topic. The series eventually won an American Bar Association Gavel Award.

The public relations people we have mentioned up to this point are all full-time professionals who have years of experience. But the public affairs chairpersons of local organizations can accomplish much the same results by following our suggestions and by devoting some time to planning.

Some broadcasters are extremely civic minded people who will spend just as much time as they can spare to help local organizations. It's not unusual for a broadcaster to practically outline a public relations campaign for a local activity, leaving the shirtsleeves work to the organization's volunteers.

There are some things you can do to prepare yourself, when you are invested with the responsibility of carrying an organization's message to the public.

First, determine just how many broadcast stations serve the area you need to cover. Start your list by putting down the ones you know. Then check newspaper radio and TV listings for the call letters of other stations which may serve the area. Check your telephone directory white pages, under "W" for states east of the Mississippi and under "K" west of the Mississippi. Some of the stations will be outside your area and will simply have business phones listed in your directory.

You can call or write your state broadcasters association. A quick call to the manager of any local station will get you the address and phone number. The association will give you the specifics you need, including up-to-date addresses and phone numbers, and the names of station managers. You should consult the broadcasters association early in your planning since some associations have only part-time staffs, and may take a while to respond.

Check your membership rolls to see if personnel from any of the local stations—or their spouses—belong. If so, contact these individuals and ask if they can spend a little time with you establishing contacts and suggesting whom to approach for what.

Check the program listings in the newspapers for public affairs programs. Also watch and listen, so that you can become acquainted with the programming of the stations you wish to contact.

Consult with the staff of other civic organizations. They may be able to share information they've already collected.

Establish a list of objectives. If you want to ask for spot announcements promoting an event or a fund drive, then you will want to contact the person in charge of public service announcements. If you have the skill or have someone who can help you, prepare the announcements ahead of time. If not, many stations will assist you, if you approach them in plenty of time to allow for the preparation of necessary materials.

If you want to suggest guests for interviews on public affairs programs, you need to contact either the program director or the public affairs director. If you think you have an idea for a possible news story or news feature, you will want to contact the news director (or at a large station, the assignment editor).

You should be alert for the names of these people. They often get mentioned on the air and in the papers, and everytime you hear or see someone identified whom you feel is an appropriate contact, write the name down.

The best way to make a cold contact at a station is to call the general manager. Through the manager or his secretary, you will be able to determine, specifically, whom you should be talking to about your needs. Then follow up by talking with these key individuals, briefly—probably on the phone first, and later in a short face-to-face meeting.

One special tip: In some areas one or more broadcast stations run annual or semi-annual seminars for civic organizations. These sessions outline the possible resources at the station, some requirements which stem from FCC rules and regulations and from production limitations, and usually, some valuable how-to-do-it tips.

Be certain that your organization sends one or more people to these seminars, if they are available. Many stations use these same meetings to assist in their obligation to ascertain community needs, and you may find yourself being interviewed by a station representative so that the station can develop programming attuned to your community.

As a public relations representative, there are a few practical realities you must face. First, understand what is "news." The majority of the stories on local newscasts deal with events affecting the community at large, or special groups within the community and with what your local government is doing for the residents. There are stories about the courts and what actions they have taken, about social issues, about consumer frauds or the misbehavior of public officials. Your local news department is really an ombudsman for you, keeping an eye on the conduct of government and probing into what helps and hinders the quality of life in your community.

Your local news department is not—in the eyes of professional journalists—an outlet for the promotion of money-making ventures, specific fund drives or opinion-forming campaigns.

Therefore, don't expect the news director of a local station to jump for joy just because you call and say you are having a luncheon to kick off the annual civic betterment campaign. The news director knows that, frankly, very few of his listeners or viewers outside the group attending will care about the luncheon. The news director is far more interested in seeing what you are doing with the money collected, and what sort of civic betterment projects you plan to do with the money you are collecting. If your form of civic betterment involves *doing* something, your local news director will be interested in taping interviews or filming while the activity is underway. Basically, you have to demonstrate that the public's money is used wisely and for needed purposes. Do this, and you should get the news coverage, because you are doing something which will have an effect on the community as a whole.

The same rule of thumb applies when you approach a public affairs director with the suggestion that someone from your organization be interviewed. The public affairs director will want to know what your organization has been done in the past, and why it is important that it collect funds.

You should suggest guests who are fully informed on the topics you expect to have discussed. This may take the highest degree of diplomacy on your part, because the top echelon of your organization may not necessarily include the best choices for interviewees. If you keep showing up at local broadcast stations with guests who can't handle a substantial interview, you will soon find yourself persona non grata.

One other important piece of advice. DO NOT give the producer or interviewer a list of suggested questions. You are insulting their intelligence and professional skill. It may be that your questions will be better than theirs, but you can't expect any cooperation from people if you go around crushing their egos!

Don't expect the reporters and interviewers whom you deal with to share all of your attitudes regarding your organization. They may ask some terribly hard-nosed, and perhaps (if you're not prepared), embarrassing questions. You must recall that they ask the same hard-nosed questions of the people whom you elect to spend your tax money!

Or, to put it another way, what some would call "back-patting" interviews are on the way out. There are so many demands on public affairs time, and so many stations are now programming public affairs shows in high listener and viewer times, that they must provide solid, substantial, interesting guests and topics to keep their audience's attention.

Bob VanWagoner, who handles ConRail public relations in the New York metropolitan area has two good hints for public relations people:

"We work to mesh smoothly with broadcast media by being available, being responsive, being candid, and being succinct."

Herbert Hands of the American Society of Civil Engineers had these thoughts on his role: "My philosophy is...that I consider myself as a member of their (the media's) staff, ready, willing, and able to assist them in getting a good story..... I must suggest an idea, different approaches, and have background information ready to support story ideas. I must also have suggestions as to physical facilities, availability of persons to conduct the story and be of practical assistance in every possible way."

Hands continued: "In all of this one should be knowledgeable in what the media is or should be looking for and what normal requirements may be desired. Thus I have found that the best techniques in securing placements are personal contact, full knowledge, suggestion of ideas, appreciation of needs and willingness to follow through with all possible assistance."

Jim Warren at the National Kidney Foundation says: "I find that the only method that consistently works is by making the suggestions personally." Warren seldom sends blind news releases, and when he does he tries to follow up with a telephone call.

The Director of Public Information at Old Sturbridge Village, a restoration of early rural New England, was Larry Morrison. Morrision prefers to get placements on programs. He says Old Sturbridge Village seeks air time for crafts demonstrators. Morrison elaborated: "Old Sturbridge Village, interpreting as it does the work, family and community life of rural New England, five or six generations ago, offers many insights and contrasts with life in America today. For example, the world of early 19th century women makes a good women's talk show subject, perhaps combined with a demonstration of spinning or weaving or candledipping. We do that sort of thing."

Morrison has another reminder—he sends thank you notes to stations which they can put in their FCC files.

HOW TO DO IT

One item which public relations people sometimes overlook is physical facilities. If a radio or television reporter is coming to do an interview, find out what type of surroundings will be best.

For radio a quiet room with fairly dull acoustics will help for an interview. Be aware of one very troublesome problem of offices and industrial buildings. You often have sources of ambient noise which are troublesome, and can ruin an audiotape. There are noisy air conditioning outlets that put a sound in the background of a tape which can virtually ruin it, ringing telephones, public address and background music systems, machinery (inside and outside), office noises, or construction sounds.

Try to find ways to overcome these. If necessary move to a different office. If possible find a location where the radio reporter can sit close to the interviewee, say a couch, or across the corner of a conference table. Executive desks are sometimes a problem, because even though the reporter draws up to the desk corner, the executive may rock back in his or her swivel chair and go off mike or cause the recording to have uneven sound levels.

Many radio reporters want to collect ambient sound—the sounds of activity related to your business or function—without having voices on the tape. Be prepared to take the reporter or producer into interesting areas where this sound can be recorded. You might dry run your place by walking around—with a battery-operated tape recorder if you have one.

In radio, sound has to be obvious to be effective. The noise of a crowd can be indistinguishable from the noise of a windstorm. But if you record the crowd in a department store, so that you can hear cash registers working and sales clerks talking, the crowd noise takes on meaning, orientation. The same is true for a hospital. People have become so used to hospital public address systems being used on radio and television, that one way to establish your locale is to record some hallway sound with the public address system in the background.

In television, your problems multiply. All that has been said about radio sound applies as well to television sound. But add these problems: lighting, background, power sources, set-up.

Many public relations experts find that the best way to set up a television interview is to provide the crew with a location which meets their technical needs—perhaps a conference room with even lighting and a good background wall. Let the crew set up, adjust their lights and microphones, and then bring in the interviewee. This is less irritating to the person being interviewed. It allows for a much smoother operation, rather than trying to introduce the subject to reporter or producer, while one or two technicians make the necessary adjustments.

Keep in touch with technical advances in the media. Find out about requirements for film cameras and electronic news cameras.

Fig. 8-1. Live television coverage of the launch of Apollo 14. The media rely heavily on business and government public relations people during this type of coverage, which involves both security considerations and a great deal of highly technical information. (Photo courtesy of Philips Broadcast Equipment Corp.)

There are differences, and you will be way ahead of the game, if you know some of the technical requirements to help out in selecting the location for the interview (Fig. 8-1).

A note about electronic news gathering equipment. Some stations are using a small window sill transmitter to relay the signal from the interview camera to a remote truck outside. Learn where the stations you deal with (which have this equipment) park their mobile vans; (they choose a location suitable for a live relay to the TV station). And find out what windows in the key parts of your building best serve as relay points. Knowing little facts like this will endear you to the television folks.

Be sure to select an interview location away from exterior windows, because they cause light problems, especially with color film. The variations in the nature, quality and quantity of exterior and interior light wrecks havoc on color film. Do not place your interviewee against a window, since he or she will be asked to move anyway. Most of these matters can be worked out in a few minutes, if you talk with the reporter or producer before the visit.

Some of today's equipment runs entirely on batteries, so check beforehand to see if the crew will need electric power.

If they do, be sure there is electric power available at a convenient distance. If there is none, perhaps your maintenance department can provide a heavy-duty extension cord or outlet box. And be concerned about where power cables will have to be run. You don't want to create any office safety hazards.

Learn a little about backgrounds. Most producers won't want to shoot against a mirror, due to the confusion of images and lighting and focus problems. Visualize the background which will be behind the interviewee. You don't want a piece of statuary, or a plant or part of a picture growing out of your person's head, when the interview is shown on TV. Think about curtains, too. Some of the worst visual settings seen on television are interviews that have had to be done in hotel ballrooms or against motel curtains—which for some reason have universally ugly patterns or colors when seen on TV.

Remove unnecessary objects—then check to see if you've done more harm than good. All too often a picture is taken down, exposing a section of wall that is lighter and cleaner than the surrounding wall!

You will build valuable bonds of friendship with the broadcast media, if you work out these problems beforehand. Most reporters, producers and crews are very busy and they like to spend a maximum amount of time talking to the interviewee, rather than having to set up and arrange their equipment.

About copies of interviews. Most stations—for reasons having to do with freedom of press issues—will not release copies or originals of material not actually broadcast. They will probably never release the original copies of material used on the air, because it needs to be kept on file for legal reasons.

Radio stations will sometimes provides copies of aired interviews, if time allows, since this is a quick and inexpensive procedure. Stations which have the personnel available, will occasionally even provide transcripts.

Television stations are less likely to provide copies of interviews just because (1) the videotape needed is expensive, (2) time and facilities needed for this type of activity are very limited.

Most stations will be very cooperative about letting you know when the interview is going to be used, but good follow through on your part is still a wise policy.

You should alert your personnel or membership to listen and watch. The station will appreciate the added little mention in your newsletter or employee publication. And, of course, you will want your organization to have tangible evidence that you have been doing your job.

THOUGHTS FOR BROADCASTERS—FROM PR PEOPLE

In our research into what public relations people do to gain access to broadcast time, we came across a number of pet peeves which translate into do's and don'ts for broadcasters. The suggestions we incorporate herein are designed to smooth relations for public affairs people and may well apply rather broadly to all public activities of broadcasters.

There is a misconception that broadcasting is a glamorous field and that the broadcaster will become self-important. The broadcaster, in his own way, is a public servant. He gains the ability to conduct his activities through a government franchise, which clearly demands that he serve his coverage area and continually work to improve that service through good public contacts.

Then there's the sales side of the issue. What your account executives don't need are enemies. The person you insult through boorish behavior may well influence a potential or existing account, thus taking money out of the station, and indirectly limiting the public affairs budget.

The broadcasters owe the public courtesy and consideration.

One public relations specialist put it this way: He dislikes "promises made by stations to show up, but when they don't show, there is no advance notification that they couldn't make it; or no notification at all when they show up at a (convention) news room and want to interview someone, whom I can't or have great difficulty in locating...."

Public relations people understand that all appointments can't be kept, and they are used to smoothing ruffled feathers within their organizations. But its hard to soothe a boss who has waited for a reporter to show up beyond the appointed time. Even a few minutes notice gives the public relations representative time to finesse the cancellation and leave the door open for a later visit.

The second part of the comment—sudden drop-ins—really hits on another issue. Some broadcasters are appallingly crude, rude and impolite. Sadly enough, the same criticism sometimes goes for technical crews when they express boredom or frustration in loud and clear language, making everyone uncomfortable and hurting the image of their employer. When you are on a film or ENG crew, there are periods of inactivity; some of it is unavoidable, but nothing is gained by insulting everyone around.

On the other hand, some crews do their stations a great deal of good because the members are naturally polite, naturally interested in people, and frequently, end up in conversations with the people they are visiting. On more than one occasion a friendly, convivial crew member has paved the way for greater cooperation. Sometimes crew members come up with solid news or documentary tips, just because they are polite and friendly.

It's a team operation for the broadcasters involved!

Frances Griffin, who directed the public information activities of Old Salem, a Moravian restoration in North Carolina, made another good point.

"All too often, the program people decide what they want and insist on doing it when they want to. In an operation such as ours, which is open to the public and in which we try to faithfully follow an authentic line of interpretation, this can be very irritating. Our buildings are tied up, often at the busiest visitor times. The interpretation that the TV programmers put on whatever gimmick they have thought up, is often contrary to the story we are trying to tell. We try to cooperate, but a little more consideration by the stations of our problems and purposes would certainly make working together more pleasant."

ConRail representative Bob VanWagoner has had the unenviable task of representing a decrepit commuter rail system undergoing a rapid and expensive revitalization.

VanWagoner has some observations on what happens in this sort of situation. "As commuter operations did improve—and, in some area and over some periods, substantially—I learned that the media, in general, are slow to free old, familiar whipping boys. I carried around, on my person, sets of statistics on various aspects of the train operations, including those which showed significant progress. Unfortunately, I found few occasions when the media was interested in this comparison and evidence; and in fact, more often, they acted threatened that I was taking something away from them—a patsy for criticism and derision."

One can understand that given this sort of situation, it was very difficult for news or documentary reporters to obtain significant interviews with ConRail's top management.

VanWagoner had one other observation which is most worthy of mention. "If on-air personnel followed more closely the material provided them by their reporters, researchers or newswriters, a more accurate and proper picture would be given the public.

"Everytime a piece of budding news is treated with a new attitude, or attempt at flair, it stands another chance of being distorted."

VanWagoner is saying that we must not let our predispositions cloud our unbiased reporting of the facts as we discover them. This is true of all reporting, whether it be spot news, or a documentary.

One way in which stories, interviews and documentaries get distorted is for the broadcaster to assume that the facts and attitudes taken by some other source or publication are absolute.

Let's face it, a good number of stories developed for mini-documentaries and their full-length counterparts, and many of the questions used on interviews are the result of wire service or newspaper or magazine stories.

Check the facts. Say to your contact, "You were quoted as saying thus and so, is this accurate?" Check the facts and figures, explore the attitudes. Sometimes you will find differences of interpretation between the source you consulted and the statements made by the person you contact. These may be errors or discrepancies brought on by omission. Occasionally, the preceding reporter or writer may have approached the story from a specific point of view, arranging the facts and interpretation fo fulfill certain expectations. So much of an interview never gets into print or into a finished program, that there is always going to be a question about whether what is quoted completely represents the statement of the person interviewed.

It also doesn't make sense for you to be doing a line for line rehash of something you've already read. You should be developing the story differently, applying it to your specific local situation, or presenting it in what you feel is a more complete or more accurate light.

Larry Morrison of Old Sturbridge Village has an important reminder for broadcasters: "A concern I have is the lack of preparation most talk show personalities have in interviewing people.... We always provide, in advance, a package of our material which, I imagine, the host thumbs through. Hosts, of course, usually ask decent questions. But the listeners and viewers could get much, much more from the program if the host would bone up more thoroughly."

Jim Warren of the National Kidney Foundation has a similar comment: "Television coverage of a news-type event, more often than not, will disrupt the event with their equipment and need for short, rather surface answers. That is just the nature of the beast and we have to work with it."

There will always be public relations representatives who are irritating, either because they bring in ideas which are totally unuseable, or take up unnecessary time, but the wise public affairs person learns how to make best use of some very fine services which are available.

This means, in many cases, working with your public relations contacts, helping them to understand your problems better and stimulating them to think of ways in which they can be more helpful.

Chapter 9
Public Information:
Governmental Public Information

In the preceding chapter we discussed the work and roles of public relations representatives of commercial and non-profit organizations.

This chapter deals exclusively with public relations as practiced—or as should be practiced—in government at all levels.

People who represent governments and governmental units carry a variety of titles. They are known as public affairs directors, public information officers, or communications officers, among other designations.

A highly-placed federal public information officer supplied us with his definitions of three functions a government representative performs. They are:

Publicity—stunts staged to gain short term newspaper or broadcast radio mention for a person or product.

Public Relations—a series of considered efforts to have a person or organization conduct activities in ways to gain positive exposure in the media and a favorable public reception over more than the short term.

Public Affairs—informational and service activities of governmental groups for public benefit over the long term.

The same public officer also said:

"To underscore the differences—that are quite real—understand that what I'm really trying to have these definitions clarify is that *publicity* is meant here to be essentially aggressive, short term activity of little worth; PR is the opposite (just as people in carnivals are from the street, people in circuses are from or of the theatre). But *public affairs* is in total contrast to both because the raison d'etre is political, not profit and, therefore, the philosophical base or mode must first be defensive, not offensive."

Many government organizations are in the peculiar position of running the least well publicized and, yet, the most intensively covered of all activities, especially those of the White House, Pentagon, and State Department.

The public meetings and public documents of governmental units get careful and thorough scrutiny from the local press, while major portions of their activities go unnoticed. A skilled reporter can find numerous intriguing stories within the activities of federal, state, county and municipal governments.

For instance—you attended the city council meeting where funds were allocated for a new computer system, but how many reporters went back to study just what is being accomplished by the system? If, for example, your station did its own local television version of CBS' "60 Minutes," it might be interesting to go through the steps with the computer operator as new equipment keeps track of tax bills, the water usage figures, the cost per vehicle of municipal police cars, etc. You could shoot tape or film to illustrate these activities.

Next, ask some questions. Is the computer speeding up billing? Does it cause the city to have a faster or higher rate of payment? Is it accurate? Is it costing more or less to bill by computer than by the previous system?

You know how much it costs to operate police cars within days after the figures are turned in. What do they mean? Is the city exploring the purchase of smaller, lighter cars? Is the computer helping to pinpoint fuel-wasting activities. (Should, for example, the police officers park their cars and go on walking beats during part of each shift?) Is the city selling off old cars before they begin costing a fortune to drive and repair?

If the computer is simply storing figures, and they are not being put to use, then it serves no useful purpose.

The type of information we have described could be made into a mini or maxi-documentary. It's a little bit dry, but an imaginative producer could come up with an interesting program. What we are saying is that the management of local government, as well as local politics, makes fascinating news and public affairs material. But there has been a great deal of the Dutch-boy and the hole in the dike approach to governmental public affairs. In other words, public relations techniques have been largely used to deal with situations which have already happened, rather than as a way to supply more information to the public.

The media would benefit from more openness and professionalism by the representatives of government, just as the media (and it's public) benefits from open meetings and open record laws.

Oddly enough, most governmental units have something positive to tell about themselves, but few succeed in getting the message across.

It is true that governments use public relations or affairs persons to block or diffuse investigations into their activities. Fortunately, they seldom succeed because an aggressive, intelligent press will not be stopped at the gate in its pursuit of the facts. The famed Watergate case is a prime example.

Federal and state "freedom of information" laws have done much to open up governmental agency meetings and files to the press. The effectiveness of these laws is largely dependent on the press, which must monitor these agencies and apply the freedom of information or "sunshine" laws, whenever it appears there is an effort to conceal or cover-up by an agency.

On the other hand, conscientious well-trained governmental public affairs representatives can be extremely helpful in providing access to key individuals, and in helping to sort out the sometimes complex activities of government departments (Fig. 9-1).

Often a skilled government public information officer will help you steer your way through the maze, leading you away from the nominal (political) spokesperson toward the more knowledgeable staff member, without leaving behind any injured egos.

Skilled government public information specialists are a big help to public affairs directors in broadcasting, because they are constantly pointing out individuals and activities of their departments, which make either good interview or good documentary material.

There is a crying need for more trained professional public information people in government, especially at the local level.

Unfortunately, the record is spotty. Many governmental units try to stumble along without any professional counsel, and then the overall coverage of their activities depends on the skill and focus of local news reporters.

All too often these governmental units find that the only coverage they get is when a controversy or scandal arises. Moreover, the service aspects of their operations usually go unheralded, leaving the public without much of the information it needs about services and regulations.

Almost as bad as ignoring the need for professional help is hiring someone's brother-in-law, or the party faithful, to promote the activities of government. As has been so often said, you get what you pay for.

There is a great deal of self interest in the hiring of public affairs specialists by governmental departments. Department heads find that they need to "sell" their programs, and advertise their most important budgetary shortcomings in order to build popular and political support for appropriations.

In recent years financially-strapped governments, especially at the local level, have found they have a vast reservoir of untapped talent, in the form of volunteers. These governments have found that they must reach out to explain their duties and needs to the public, and to encourage and then compliment the people who volunteer to serve.

Other department heads find they can dispell some criticism traditionally received by their departments by getting public affairs help, and by being open in the conduct of their affairs.

One example of the new "openness": There has been somewhat of a turnaround in some prison systems at the federal and state level. Today, many penal systems encourage media visits, often with no restrictions other than those having to do with security and the right of privacy. The Federal Bureau of Prisons has been particularly active in opening its doors to the media. Documentary producers can get access to facilities quickly and easily. Obviously, the situation is not one of total frankness, but giant steps have been made in permitting documentary and public affairs programs to be done inside federal correctional facilities.

As one government public affairs officer has noted: "Nearly all agencies or bureaus of the government are part of the executive branch.... These agencies and bureaus are *authorized* and *funded* by Congress. And what Congress gives Congress can take away. Most agencies and bureaus are reviewed by two different committees of both houses in Congress each year, too. Therefore, most bureau directors go to the Hill at least four times each year: twice for approval on what might be called 'operations' and twice for 'budget.' Next, virtually all agency or bureau directors are political appointees subject to instant dismissal.... Finally, each agency has its own constituency on the Hill.

"Therefore, a recognition of the ever-changing political atmosphere is among the first priorities of agency public affairs executives and this, in turn, tends to create among some of them, a defensive attitude or stance toward just about anything.

"The real job of the public affairs executive must be to serve the public, for his is the primary link between his agency and more than 210 million Americans. The public demands service—and they get it—in hundreds of different ways."

Here is a list of some of the typical responsibilities of a government public affairs officer: fulfilling requests for information; sending out copies of the employee newsletter; producing specially written

Fig. 9-1. Eric B. Outwater, right, deputy regional administrator of the U.S. Environmental Protection Agency's Region II Office being interviewed by John Stossel of WCBS-TV, New York. (Photo courtesy of Environmental Protection Agency).

materials for publishers of books, encyclopedias, scholarly journals, 'trade magazines,' and popular publications; fulfilling media requests, averaging dozens daily; and continuously conducting research to answer all the questions. Finally, of course, is the preparation and releasing of news releases and features, plus the taking of photographs and maintenance of a photo library. The news releases often are the 'for the record' kind, which are necessary.

One function government public affairs people fill which can be invaluable—both to their organization and to the media—is the "breaking-in" of new reporters, and producers. A skilled public information officer can help a media person learn the initial ropes around a government department. This is especially important when it comes to understanding the personal and political relationships, which are so important to the functioning of government.

Many government departments encourage on-site visits to their facilities, instead of just channeling reporters and producers to elected or appointed leaders. There are thousands of good stories to be found within government at all levels, and these on-site visits often stimulate ideas for media people.

Just as an example: various federal departments involved in energy matters will gladly introduce reporters to key personnel and suggest possible locations for possible stories. The author recalls an inquiry to a mining department within the government which led to a trip to Pikesville, Kentucky and, among other stories, a feature on how a shortage of steel roof-bolts needed to keep coal mines safe was hindering the battle against energy-crisis fuel shortages. The needed steel was being sold to other industries!

HOW IT'S DONE IN GOVERNMENT

It's not easy being a public affairs spokesperson for a government unit. All government departments are creatures of politics, both in the elective sense, and in their internal structure. You must keep the political pecking order happy, while trying to deemphasize the shortcomings and emphasize the achievements of the unit for which you speak.

Often the people with whom the government PIO deals are unaccustomed to working with the media, and are either afraid for their jobs or suspicious of the media because of a tradition of aggressive, probing investigation of government by the press.

The government public information person must understand the structure of the organization he represents. He must know what the duties of the unit or units are, and who is responsible for doing what. This means continual learning, by talking with department heads and supervisors, by interviewing specialists, and by on-site visits to the units for which he is responsible.

This need for thorough knowledge leads to a personnel problem in government public information work. Some executives prefer to select individuals who are experienced within the organization, even if they have little media experience, just because they know the structure and function of the organization. On the other hand, other executives prefer to find experienced individuals outside government, and train them in their specific functions. Either way, the person who represents a government unit has a big job ahead of them, learning their own organization, or learning how to deal with the media.

The same rule applies in dealing with the media that goes for your internal relations. Know your media people and their functions. Find out who is who in the media within your jurisdiction.

Let's set up a theoretical example. You have been assigned by the National Park Service to do public affairs work with the broadcast media in the six New England states.

First of all, obtain a current copy of Broadcasting Magazine's *Yearbook*. It is the single best directory of the broadcast media. It will tell you the call letters, facilities, executive staff, address, telephone number and, if there is one, the telex number of the stations in your area. You will also get an idea of network affiliations and formats.

No directory is perfect. Errors are made and people change jobs. So you must set up your own card file, starting with the information you get from the *Yearbook*. Then, by one means or another—personal visits, phone calls or a mail questionnaire—check the facts on each station, especially addresses and telephone numbers and the names and titles of key personnel.

Define the names you need to know. Typically, you will want to know who is the general manager, the program manager, the news director and the public affairs director. You may also want to know who handles editorials, farm broadcasts, and environmental and recreation news. Most of these names you can gather through phone calls to the station or by on-site visits to discuss the programming and structure of the station.

Be on the lookout for other key people. Find out who hosts or produces specific programs which may interest you, and make sure these people know that you are willing to help in any way they need. They can turn out to be some of your most productive contacts.

Once you have a pretty accurate card file, work like a beaver to keep it up to date and accurate. Watch the trade magazines and newspapers for job changes. Talk with people and exchange information.

As a bare minimum you should have a subscription to *Broadcasting Magazine* which is the major trade publication. Another helpful publication for its reporting of industry trends, format changes and personnel changes is *Variety*. Both should be required reading for public information specialists.

Be sure to talk with people in the field and swap information. You'll pick up many good tips on job changes and future programs from these sources.

Meet the people you are dealing with. Go to professional meetings such as meetings of state broadcasting association and professional societies (if you belong). Rub elbows, so that the media professionals will get to know you. Ask them what they need from you and take notes. Suggest story ideas and offer your assistance.

Everywhere you go, make sure you leave behind some sort of easy-to-consult reminder—your business card—or a display card which has key phone numbers, including home numbers of people the news and public affairs departments would want to contact.

Now define the services which you have to offer. Can you provide experts for interviews? Do you need to have someone available to respond to spot news situations? Are there projects within your area which need to be explained to the public? For example, are you developing a new national park, or modifying the facilities and terrain of an existing one? What are the best and more interesting activities of your organization? What activities need more public (and political) support?

206

Let's say the National Park Service, as overseer of historical sites has acquired quite a bit of expertise in the clothing worn in Civil War America, as well as the period's lifestyle. Do you have or can you get experts who can talk about this period in American history, and illustrate their conversations in sound or through pictures? Can you do studio demonstrations?

Anything with sound or pictures will perk up a public affairs director's ears. After all, no public affairs program serves its purpose if it is dull and hence, has no audience.

A little bit of showmanship is needed to assure you of air time. After all, the competition is fierce for public affairs air time. Since the Park Service remains, for the most part, fairly non-controversial, you have to concentrate on education and service as your main points of persuasion when seeking air time.

On the other hand, you have a good record for public service working for you, because the Park Service has always been known for its concern for neatness, politeness, maintaining the natural environment and a general attitude of helping the public.

Next, define your objectives. Overall, any organization has certain things it wants to get done in a year. Prior to the summer season, the Park Service may be interested in educating and informing people about its various locations and their facilities. It may be that there is a need to educate and inform people who use camper vans and camp trailers. Or you want to get certain information into the hands of hikers and back country tent campers. You will probably want to encourage the use of less well known locations, to take the pressure off the most popular sites.

Then there's the matter of goodwill. One of your jobs would be to promote sympathetic attitudes towards the Park Service, attitudes which might, in some way, reflect on key elected officials who can affect the department's budget requests and other projects.

One technique which you could employ is the use of short public service spot announcements on radio and television stations.

But your prime objective should be to get enough public affairs time to permit you to go into some detail about your projects. This involves preparation—lining up the best possible guests and, if possible, some accompanying materials for television purposes.

Let's say that your objective is to promote a relatively new national park in the wilderness of Maine. If you can possibly do it, have some color film and slides shot of the area, so that you can stimulate the interest of television viewers. Then try to locate the best possible spokesperson you can find. While this might be the park superintendent, it may turn out to be one of the rangers. You want someone who can answer all the questions tossed at them, and who will be interesting. This can be a tough assignment since the personnel whom you will be dealing with may not be especially verbal people. In addition, you have the delicate diplomatic task of getting the best spokesperson, even if the person is not an executive of the Park Service.

What are your target programs? Some broadcast stations run programs or features about outdoor life and recreation. Obviously, while their audiences may be smaller than for some other programs, the interest per viewer will be much greater.

Next, what interview programs will be interested in your topic? Generally, they will be informational programs, as opposed to the controversial. These are frequently found on the early and mid-morning schedules of television stations, and in the mid-morning and mid-afternoon schedules of radio stations.

Don't ignore public broadcasting stations. They have many more openings for the type of interviews and presentations you have in mind and their audiences, while somewhat smaller than those of commercial stations, often have a great deal of interest in the type of material you would be presenting.

Be sure to prepare the people you are going to use as guests. They should be familiarized with some of the basics of radio and television—being certain to face the microphone, no touching of microphones or equipment, where to look when doing a television interview.

If you were planning to discuss camping safety, you could round up a couple of your best people and put on a demonstration. This sort of thing should be rehearsed. It's difficult to pitch a tent in a television studio, unless you have devised special equipment for the demonstration. Also, you will have a limited amount of time available, so you have to determine if the demonstration will take too long and, if so, how you can compress it. Sometimes the best way to do a demonstration is to almost finish it before the interview takes place, and then just do a few finishing touches during the interview.

This is primarily a visual topic, so your main target would be television stations. But you may find some radio stations that will be interested in discussing the the topic, since camping has become a major recreational activity.

An aggressive public affairs person keeps a tab on stations that are doing documentary work and offers to help. Here again, don't ignore the educational stations. They are imaginative and often better budgeted than you might think. They may very well be interested in doing something about national parks.

Because the Park Service has many children among its visitors, you would consider trying to place your people on children's programs. It's an audience frequently overlooked by organizations outside broadcasting.

If you know you are interested in placing guests on programs during a certain period of time, attempt to make personal contact with the producers or the individuals responsible for "booking" (scheduling) guests. If need be, write a letter and follow up with a telephone call. You have to be an aggressive (but not pushy) salesperson for your service, if you want to get your people onto these programs.

Most of all, be sure that your office keeps close tabs on what is going on in the broadcast field in your area. Be careful that your staff treats broadcasters politely and answers their questions promptly. Service is important in every venture dealing in human relations, and service is essential to good public relations.

We have belabored our point a bit in order to give a rather detailed picture of some of the things a public information officer would be concerned about in specific practical situations.

One public information officer offers good advice. He says don't be a "reactor." All too often government public affairs people put themselves in the position of only reacting to something that has happened. This can have negative consequences. You should think positively—try to demonstrate the best aspects of your department or agency, rather than running around defending it every time a crisis arises. Explanation is not public affairs—it is public admission of all the things we've always suspected about your department anyway.

The path to creative public affairs is the same as the path to success in most ventures—you sit down and think it through and plan.

An experienced government PIO has this formula for a public affairs effort. It consists in making decisions on some basic questions. He lists them as:

What is the message?
Who is (are) the audience(s)?
What is (which are) the media?
Why and how do they want to communicate the message?
How do I help?

The same PIO described how he approached one of his major projects: "I drew up a mailing list of about 80 key (news) papers with at least one in every state, and then an 'all other' category.... It consisted of about 120 'executives' of or officials affiliated with *carefully selected* media, based on demographics. And that list was constantly refined. It was reviewed at least once a week, and rarely a week went by without a name being added or subtracted."

Our expert says his list would have surprised many observers. It had only one person at the Associated Press—a key individual. At *Time* magazine, there were two—a key person in Washington and a senior editor in New York. At ABC the government PIO had three contacts; at NBC, initially, four, later cut to two; and at CBS, a total of nine over the period of the project.

The government PIO was asked by one broadcasting network to compile a list of possible topics for some mini-documentaries. He later said: "The resulting list so impressed me that, later, I dressed it up slightly and sent it to all contacts."

One key introduction at a network news department resulted in a series of 20 features, which were repeated once, making a total of 40 exposures on prime network television time for the department involved.

This PIO has his own set of guidelines:

"I establish contacts by first thinking of a way I can help them, then calling for an appointment, then going (there) with something interesting in hand (to be left behind).

"I never had an 'idea or person' I wish 'to push,' ...I think of my responsibility as that of communicator, and all I want to do is explain what my agency represents and how it functions..."

Our PIO happens to work for a governmental unit where he can afford to lay back a bit on "pushing" people or ideas. Your technique must be adjusted to the situation.

SOME COMMENTS FROM GOVERNMENT PIO'S

Let's turn to the practical experiences of some people who do public relations for government organizations.

Michael Aun was the Public Information Officer for the United States Department of Justice, Bureau of Prisons. Due to the nature of his department's function, Aun has an extremely difficult job. He doesn't need to sell his service, in fact, his bureau has more participants than it can ideally accommodate. Aun's Bureau can stand some image polishing—and dispell the image those late night movies give you of the prison system. In fact, Aun becomes the spokesman for a social theory of government. You're more apt to hear talk or rehabilitation versus incarceration than anything else, when you deal with top level people at the USBP. Their other major concern is getting funds for newer and different facilities.

Occasionally Aun has to stick his finger in the dike, when there's a jailbreak, or a prisoner protest.

Aun infrequently solicits interviews, but he and his superior, the director, try to react promptly and positively to requests for interviews.

The Bureau permits media representatives to tour its facilities and interview prisoners. Aun acts as a clearing house for these interviews, briefing the media on the Bureau's regulations regarding media visits, and helping to pinpoint the officials who can be most helpful to producers and reporters. His is primarily a service role—aiding the wardens and other bureau officials in dealing with the media, and acting as a go-between for members of the media. Aun will suggest possible coverage in his dicussions with the media, and outline individuals with whom he thinks the media might want to talk.

In fact, the relationship between the Bureau of Prisons and the media is remarkably open, when you realize that the USBP has one of the most thankless jobs in government.

Occasionally Aun will contact the media when he has an event—such as a prisoner art exhibit.

The Environmental Protection Agency tends to get a great deal of media attention due to its function and to some of the controversies in which it has become involved (Fig. 9-2).

James R. Marshall directed the Public Affairs Division for EPA in the greater New York Area. He says that the approach in seeking air time has to be tempered to subject topicality and the geographic area. "New York City," said Marshall, "has extremely high competitiveness for air time. Keeping up-to-date on programming and editors/reporters with special interests in all the cities in our region of responsibility is a concern of ours."

Marshall goes on to say: "We organize topics and participants and also act as a clearing house in response to media requests for information. We arrange interviews or contacts for them here in our regional office and our Washington headquarters or EPA laboratories around the country. We take part in radio and TV shows, again either through our initiating a letter or phone call or the show contacting us."

Unlike the Bureau of Prisons, EPA has an idea to sell—the protection of our land, water and air resources. Often EPA is the advocate of a particular point of view, and so it is more active in seeking air time for its administrators and experts. EPA also gets requests for assistance from the media, because there is so much interest in environmental topics.

Earlier in this chapter we used the National Park Service as an example of a government department. An agency with somewhat similar responsibilities is the United States Forest Service. The Forest Service has supervisory responsibilities over nonrecreational forests and related area. These lands are open to public use and the Forest Service is greatly concerned about safety, vandalism, pollution and forest fires.

A great bulk of the department's message is carried through public service announcements. But Forest Service Public Information expert, Jerry W. Gause said most of his other activities are centered on feature and hard news stories. He said the Service seldom does public affairs talk shows.

At one time Gause did a camping program on a San Francisco radio station, which demonstrated the types of service an organization like the Forest Service can perform. It's not hard to imagine that a San Francisco station would have an audience for a program on camping, considering all the magnificent camping areas of the Pacific coast states and the Rocky Mountains which are reachable from the Bay area.

Gause said he does have some success in placing his people on television talk shows, where they usually end up discussing human interest or feature topics.

There is a basic difference in the mission of the Forest Service and the Park Service. The Park Service is responsible for much of the natural and historical heritage of the nation and is more consumer-oriented, encouraging the use of its facilities, and attempting to even out the flow of visitors to the biggest and most popular locations in favor of some of the less patronized sites.

The Forest Service deals with trees as an agricultural product and, for the most part, unspoiled wilderness, and is more concerned with preservation of the forests from carelessness—rather than encouraging more human visitors, who tend to upset the ecology of the woods anyway.

Bob Swenarton was Chief of the Bureau of Mines' Office of Mineral Information. His bureau is rather obscure due to the nature of its mission. "We are a small office in a small bureau that no longer

Fig. 9-2. A team of U.S. Environmental Protection Agency scientists and officials participating in a news conference for New Jersey media on toxic substances and carcinogens. (Photo courtesy of Enviornmental Protection Agency).

has any regulatory authority and has programs [R&D (research and development) in mining and metallurgy, and collection and analysis of mineral statistics] that do not excite a great deal of public interest."

Swenarton's role is more service oriented. He readily responds to enquiries from the media and is very helpful in directing media representatives to people who can answer questions. He has some solid advice to organizations seeking public affairs time: "Have something newsworthy, interesting, and important to say, and have a good spokesperson to say it.

"Most of the television coverage...has been as a result of some newsworthy research development, such as the operation of our College Park, Maryland plant for reclaiming mineral values from municipal wastes." Again the operating principle is the same—have a message that is newsworthy, something that affects a large segment of the public.

Although, for the most part, this book deals with live (or recorded) local public affairs programs, Swenarton points out a fact that should be held in mind by public affairs directors. His bureau has available a library of films on mining topics for use by television stations. These films can be useful to fill sudden gaps in program schedules and can be skillfully used to tie into discussion programs and other public affairs efforts. A public affairs director should be aware of some of the sources of film, as part of his or her inventory of resources, especially for stations which don't have budgets which permit a great deal of on-location shooting.

PR PEOPLE VIEW THE MEDIA

As we did in the preceding chapter, we would like to briefly go over some of the "gripes" expressed by public affairs people in hopes they will be valuable to broadcast public affairs specialists.

One government spokesperson with whom we consulted said that the media tend to overemphasize entertainment values. This is a fairly common criticism of broadcasting, and stems partly from a misunderstanding of the basic concept of broadcasting (as we practice it in this country) compared to that of our newspapers. For the most part broadcasting is an entertainment medium, although this concept is changing. Newspapers have been primarily informers, although they now tend to print more feature and entertainment material.

Stephen Bennett was director of the Public Information Office for Forsyth County, North Carolina. He had an interesting comment on broadcast coverage by television stations in his area. The television market which includes Forsyth County also includes another major population center, in adjacent Guilford County. There are three major television stations serving the two counties, one in Forsyth and two in Guilford. Bennett said: "The main problem has been the stations which supposedly serve our area...but that are physically located in other cities... (They) do not feel as inclined to present public service broadcasting as does the local affiliate..."

Broadcasters should take note of one criticism which frequently originates from people in government is the lack of preparation on the part of reporters. It's difficult to ask good questions and not waste the time of the interviewee if you are ill-prepared. Careless or inaccurate editing of tape and film, can also significantly change the meaning of what was said in an interview.

One federal official gripes that he gets last minute requests for interviews and finds some interviewers poorly briefed. Obviously, on hard news topics last minute interviews can be unavoidable, but certainly for most public affairs and documentary projects there is no excuse for last minute arrangements and poor preparation, except the lack of thought and organization on the part of the producer.

From the viewpoint of broadcasters, the major problems which stem from dealing with government representatives revolve around the representatives' lack of understanding of the media, or simple bureaucratic inefficiency. Bureaucrats tend to want to put it off until tomorrow (maybe it will go away); check it with the chief (I'm up for a GS-13); do a little research (who does the boss want to stick with this one?); or defer to another entity (oh, my God, Congressman Oligarchy will come down on us if we talk about this one!).

These problems aren't easy to solve for those who work in government, but they have been overcome by some public information people, and the results in the form of media coverage have been noteable.

Chapter 10
Reporting Your Good Works

Our final chapter could be called "The Rewards and How You Reap Them."

Gaining recognition for your hard work on public affairs programs is an important part of the total job of being a public affairs director or producer.

Our concerns in this chapter are twofold: First, how to gain recognition for our good works, and second, telling others about the awards. It's part of the total cycle of broadcasting, which includes producing a topnotch product, testing it in the marketplace, and telling everyone just how well you are doing.

AWARDS AND HOW TO GO AFTER THEM

There's great satisfaction in listening to or viewing one of your public affairs programs and saying to yourself, "Gee, that was great."

But there's even more satisfaction from having someone else tell you what a terrific job you've done.

And after everyone's over the ego trip, there's the all-important prestige and promotional opportunities, which accrue from being recognized for the quality of your programming.

Every station manager, news director, public affairs director, program director should be alert for opportunities to compete for recognition of the station's public affairs programming.

There are many benefits to be gained from winning awards. They enhance the station's stature in the community, and in the profession. This can mean more audience and more sales.

It can mean that better job applicants will apply, feeling that the station is an important step in their careers.

Some prizes have monetary value, which can be used to reward creative employees, or buy vitally-needed equipment.

Winning awards enhances the professional and social prestige of the management and staff—which can be very important in the inner political workings of the community, and equally as important in the political workings of professional societies.

More than one station enjoys a top reputation, not through its day to day excellence, but through recognition it has achieved for specific accomplishments. If you stop to think, you will realize that many of the stations which enjoy wide reputations are comparable to or even less well programmed, than stations which aren't well known. Often the difference is skillful promotion—which includes gaining local, regional and national recognition for public affairs and news programming.

Later on in this chapter we will provide a listing of many of the awards which are open to public affairs programs.

At this point, we would like to discuss winning these awards.

We'll assume you design and produce the program first, and then think about its award-winning possibilities later. This is putting your priorities in the right order. No program should be produced, just because it has the potential to be a prize winner. But every program should be evaluated as a possible award applicant.

What are some of the categories to consider? First of all, documentaries are excellent candidates for recognition. Editorials come next, and then special public affairs programs, followed by regularly-scheduled public affairs programs. There are even awards which recognize the overall balance of a station's public affairs and news activity.

Uniqueness is the way. A unique idea always has a foot up on the ladder when you apply for prizes. For example, it was fairly easy for the CBS Radio Network to draw attention to its mini-documentary series when it began, because the form was relatively unused in radio, especially in network radio. Now radio mini-docs are commonplace.

Quality is another key. The better the work, the more creative the product; the more incisive the questions, the better your chances of being honored.

The topical nature of the subject matter is important. Award juries perk up in response to topics of current interest, especially if you can show they relate to your community. This is why it sometimes seems as if there has been a run on documentaries about alcoholism, or abortion, or some other topic.

After Watergate stations started winning prizes for uncovering malfeasance in their local governments.

Think about who is likely to be interested in your program. If it is extraordinarily good, or you have a solid, broad-range program or overall programming, then aim for the top—the Peabody, The RTNDA awards, the SPJ-SDX (Society of Professional Journalist-Sigma Delta Chi) awards, etc.

Aim for target groups. If your topic deals with legal matters, submit applications to the American Bar Association Gavel awards and to similar groups. There are many special interest groups who, each year, honor stations for programming which deals with their concerns.

Think on several levels. It is conceivable for a program to be honored at the state level—say a wire service association award; at the national level—say the SPJ-SDX award; and perhaps by a special interest group. Many of the top national submissions win multiple awards.

Think not only about specific programs and series, think about your station's overall image. A number of stations have been honored because they made a total commitment to public affairs, rather than because any one element was extraordinary. It's one of the few cases where you can receive recognition for doing your everyday job well.

While it is a little easier for the well-staffed, wealthy station to fare well in award competitions, small and understaffed stations should not shy away. Most award juries take into consideration how well you have done in relation to your facilities, resources and community size, when they consider the overall quality of your product.

And that's exactly why some small stations end up winning big awards.

Regardless of anything else, small stations should compete actively for the specialized awards and for local, state and regional awards, where the judges are apt to be even more understanding about the difficulties under which small stations work.

You stand a better chance of winning many award competitions, if you understand the inner workings of the group to whom you are applying. For instance, things will go a little smoother when you apply for an award granted by a professional association, if members of your staff belong to and are somewhat active in that association. Reasons: the recognition factor and you can find out what standards the organization will use in judging you.

The same rule applies when seeking recognition from major interest groups. If your staff is known to the organization's top echelon and its public affairs staff, you will be able to get some helpful hints on what to submit and how. There have even been instances where organizations have suggested applications to producers, because they perceived a need for more and better applicants in certain categories.

Packaging is important in applying for awards. Take the time to fill out applications carefully. Spend the time and effort to provide neat, typed transcripts of program material. Make sure copies of exhibits are neat. And of course, use high-quality materials, if you send audiotape or videotape. The latter is an expensive item, but it is well worth the investment, if you honestly think you have a strong candidate for a major award.

You should involve your publicity or public relations staff, because they may be able to offer useful suggestions on packaging the entry. In addition, they should know what awards you are seeking, so that appropriate follow-up publicity can be distributed, if you win.

Okay, you get the word you've won an award. As soon as the awarding organization issues its press release, either issue your own, or see that the organization's release gets to the right sources.

Duplicate coverage of local, state and regional media. The awarding organization may have overlooked someone, and there's a tendency to throw out national press releases without reading them. That's why you should reissue the release, and follow up with telephone calls to make sure it is read.

Think about the publicity outlets with which the national organization would not be familiar. If, for example, you have done a program which wins an award from the American Bar Association, make sure that the release is repeated in publications of organizations to which the people you interviewed belong. It's a big ego trip for your interviewees, and will make you friends who can be helpful at other times. Put someone on a prize-winning program and you have a friend for life! Even though the Bar association will have sent along notices to the state and local Bar associations, check to make sure their newsletters are going to mention the award.

Getting your station mentioned in specialized newsletters, magazines, employee publications and the like gets attention for you on a much more personalized basis. Often, the readers of these publications do not customarily discern your station from the dozens of others they encounter.

Make sure the professional organizations to whom the program's producer, talent, writer and other staff belong know about the award. You should inform the alumni associations at the colleges these people attended. It's a good way to have it known in the trade that you are doing a topnotch job, and alumni magazines, especially, can stimulate enquiries from potential future employees. Most professional organizations have magazines or newsletters with sections set aside for notes about the achievements of their members. Make sure your staff gets mentions. It means a great deal to a hardworking staff member to get recognition from his peers.

Take out media ads, if your award is important enough. It may cost a few bucks, but if it helps media buyers and other ad agency people to remember you a little better, this advertising could be good for business. Your station representative will love you.

Be sure to tell the public in your audience area. Mention the award on your own air, and buy advertisements in the local print media. Pat yourself on the back, it's good business.

Most stations hang their award certificates and plaques in locations where they will be seen by the public. One common location is the main reception area. It gives visitors something to stare at, and leaves them with the impression that you have a great concern for your community. Other locations include the general manager's office, the news director's office, the public affairs director's office and the program director's office.

One pet peeve from the author. Remove awards you won years ago. There is something less than impressive about sitting in an uncomfortable waiting room, staring at a station's 1959 Red Cross Appreciation Award.

It's hard to imagine that any one would overlook it, but you should organize the information about prizes you have won for public affairs type programming, so that it can be considered for inclusion with exhibits for your renewal application. After all, prizes are a demonstrable example of the quality of your public affairs programming.

One policy matter which should be decided ahead of time, if your station is actively seeking to win awards for its public affairs programming, is how any prize money will be used.

Some stations split the money among the people who actually produced the program. Others apply it towards equipment needed to do public affairs programming. Some channel the money to a charity in the station's name. A great deal of turmoil can be created while management vacillates over what to do with a $1,000 prize check.

Another idea—why not repeat the prize-winning program (with appropriate mention that it won a prize), so that more people will have an opportunity to hear or see it.

OUTSIDE NON-BROADCAST ACTIVITIES

Station managers and public affairs directors should spend some time analyzing the station's participation in the community—other than in its broadcast activities.

Members of the staff and management often play very important roles in the community, in ways which never result, directly, in on-air programming.

A television reporter, assigned to cover a specific community, once advised the mayor and city fathers on how to promote a parade and day of ceremonies honoring a Congressional Medal of Honor winner. This included ghost writing press releases and radio and TV spots to stimulate community attendance at the event. The reporter instructed the city fathers on how to approach various media to solicit their support in promoting and covering the event. The reporter built a great deal of good will for the station and enhanced his standing with a number of influential community leaders, through his private efforts. The station eventually received letters of thanks for insertion in its FCC files.

This type of community participation is common to the everyday activities of the station and sales managers, as well as the news and public affairs directors. Many times stations have community affairs and editorial directors, who spend a great deal of time helping the community in ways which do not directly result in programming.

It's good to take stock occasionally, and see how good a citizen your station is. Sincere management personnel would want to be deeply involved in the community—for both altruistic and business reasons. If a community is important enough to live in, and to do business in, it is important enough to participate in!

Anything you do to make the community more prosperous, a better place to live, attractive to business, etc., is good business. After all, the station's income is derived from advertising, and most advertising is for products and services which are offered in competition within the community, or are above the level of a person's most essential needs.

How do station owners, managers and executives and their staffs participate in the community?

You should have the answer to this in the station's files. A part of the information stations gather for license renewal time includes the civic affiliations of their staff.

Let's look at some possibilities:

The Chamber of Commerce, Better Business Bureau
Churches and Temples
The Council of Churches
The Anti-Poverty Agency Board of Directors
The Parent-Teachers Association
Boy and Girl Scouts, Camp Fire Girls
The YMCA, YWCA, the YMHA
Boys Club, Girls Club
Fraternal Organizations
Optomists, Rotary, Lions, Toastmasters
Retail Merchants Association

United Fund, Salvation Army, Red Cross
Little League
Big Brothers and Big Sisters
Orphanage Board of Directors
Elective and Appointive Civic Offices
Community Development Council
NAACP, CORE
State and Regional Advisory Groups
Volunteer Fire Department, Rescue Squad, Auxiliary Police
Community Center Board of Directors
Hospital Board, Hospital Volunteer
Veterans Groups
Symphony Society, Barbershop Quartet, Choir

Our list could extend almost into infinity. The point is—the station, and its staff, participate in many, many aspects of the community, and you should (1) have this information on file, and (2) encourage this sort of activity.

One of the unique qualities of broadcasting is the feeling of community—that the station is usually thought of as a part of the community—and that working for the station generally brings with it a degree of admiration from friends, relatives, neighbors and other people in the community.

Through this network of community participants, you can be gathering ideas for public affairs programming, for news coverage, and occasionally, ideas for potential sponsors.

Let's talk about some specific examples of non-broadcast activities by stations:

In many communities, radio and television stations have become clearinghouses to solve consumer and other problems. Sometimes a few of these problems are selected as examples to be used on the air by consumer or "action" reporters, to show how problems can be solved. But in a number of cases, the service is offered without any direct relationship to any on-air programming.

A typical situation would be for a station to install a special telephone number for the public to call with problems. Solving these problems sometimes involves cutting bureaucratic red tape, getting refunds for merchandise, finding a specialized service such as a homemaker for an invalid, or unraveling a computer screw-up.

Some stations recruit volunteers to staff these services. Sometimes the calling hours are limited to relatively brief periods, so the phones can be adequately staffed. Some stations work with municipal and county consumer affairs departments, to inform the public on ways to overcome typical problems. Others simply write a covering letter to accompany the material from the complainant, and see that the matter gets to the attention of the proper agency or organization for resolution. Most broadcast stations know or can find the right persons or agencies to get someone working on the solution of these problems.

Various organizations doing this sort of work report wide differences in their success in solving problems. Among the stumbling blocks: a lack of desire to solve the problem by the organization consulted, and bureaucratic backlogs that make it nearly impossible to speed up processing.

In some cases, a lot depends on how much clout the station wishes to exert. If the station is simply acting as a clearinghouse, it is serving, primarily, as a semi-skilled dispatcher of complaints. If the station airs some of the problems received and tells how they were resolved, it has the added muscle of being able to say to a recalcitrant organization—either you solve this person's problem, or we go on the air and discuss all your dirty linen in public. This approach, while harsh, is apt to gain the needed cooperation. Like all weapons, it must be used judiciously and infrequently to be most effective.

In March 1976, the *New York Times* surveyed the various "Action" services in the New York Metropolitan area. Five radio and TV stations were identified as having this sort of service. The number of complaints received by the stations varied from as low as 200 per week up to a high of 1,000 per week.

Two of the five broadcast outlets accepted telephone calls and the other three accepted only letters. The staffs, usually a mixture of paid and volunteer workers ranged from a low of three to a high of 120. Three of the five stations used the telephone to attempt to resolve complaints, the other two sent form letters.

Broadcast stations throughout the country participate actively in charity projects—especially those which tie in well with programming and personalities.

Karen King of KKUA Radio in Honolulu said: "KKUA has taken part in several major charity projects including Project Concern's

Walk for Mankind, the Cystic Fibrosis Bike-A-Thon, American Cancer Society drives, Easter Seals shows, and...Muscular Dystrophy programs."

Ms. King gave a specific example: "Project Concern's Walk for Mankind was the most successful in the Project's history. The Walk was 20 miles long, over 10,000 people walked, and over $200,000 in contributions and pledges were collected. All of our disc jockeys and heartier members of the staff particpated, with disc jockeys making live reports at different stages of the walk. Prior to the Walk, KKUA Walk for Mankind tee-shirts were awarded on the air and made available, later, to all walkers."

It's an example of community participation which made use of the station's "aura" to heighten interest in the charity event—and, at the same time, promoted the station—as an involved member of the community.

A Florida radio station reported that it loans its disc jockeys each year for a local television station's telethon. This cooperative arrangement has gone on for a number of years.

A good many stations actively seek to have their personalities participate in public fund raising events. It's a good way to stimulate good will and help ensure the success of the event at the same time.

Sometimes stations will foot the bill for bumper stickers or buttons, or share their billboards or transit advertising with worthwhile community causes.

At Christmastime, a number of radio stations hold on and off-air auctions to raise funds for social service organizations. One longstanding effort is undertaken annually by WBZ Radio in Boston. The station traditionally broadcasts from a mobile studio located on the Boston Common. People passing by and listeners are invited to bid on or pay set prices for certain items and services. The money goes to the "700 Fund" to help needy families.

Loaning facilities is a common activity. One radio station in North Carolina will send out its flat-bed trailer to community events. The trailer is used as a bandstand and as a platform from which children's games and contests are directed.

Other stations loan members of their news or public affairs staffs to help moderate debates or discussions.

Radio stations sometimes provide public address facilities.

The majority of stations are willing to provide advisory services to organizations, telling them how to promote their activities, how to organize guests for interviews, how to stage skits or demonstrations, etc.

One Connecticut television station scheduled regular seminars for public affairs chairpersons. Every civic group known to the station was invited to send representatives to a seminar on using the media to tell their story. The seminars concentrated on how to use the broadcast media, what the media expects from the groups, basics of broadcast techniques, writing and visualization for broadcast media, and whom to contact. The station developed a manual which it distributed to each participant.

The station gained from the project by coming into contact with more groups and by "educating" these groups, as to what could and couldn't be done with available facilities and time, and how to organize for public affairs programs. The seminars saved a lot of wasted time for both sides in later meetings, since each side had developed some basic understanding of each others resources.

Some stations throw their doors open to the community by providing space for civic meetings—whether it be a conference room, an unused studio or a hall. Even a small radio station can make the public welcome, by being friendly and helpful to everyone who comes in person, and by offering to help out in little ways, such as sponsoring a coffee and doughnut breakfast while local women's club presidents hold a planning session.

Bill O'Shaughnessy of WVOX in New Rochelle, New York recounted one incident which involved his station. "We had a situation," he said, "where we had a three to two majority in the city council, and the mayor was in the minority. And they were bickering and they couldn't agree on anything...so I had a quiet little lemonsqueeze for about, turned out to be 93 guys or something; locked them in a room at the...country club...and didn't let them out of the room...finally the five councilmen and the chairman of the Republican Party went out of there, hand in hand, with the chairman of the Democratic Party. The first time those guys had spoken in more than a year."

O'Shaughnessy said the session was completely off the record, and no report of it or any of the matters discussed was broadcast. He felt the action by the station was needed to overcome a civic logjam.

O'Shaughnessy said his station once interceded to get the mayor of one city in the service area together with the board chairman of a giant utility to work out what was to be done with a piece of property, which had been the subject of a long-running controversy.

Another area in which many stations are active, but which gets no on-air mention is education. Almost every station, at one time or another, provides people to talk to groups of students, or to conduct guided tours. Some provide rooms for class meetings and laboratory work.

Most stations willingly conduct tours through their facilities. Some have developed set presentations, with staff members designated to conduct the tours, and special materials which they give the visitors.

In other cases the process is more informal, with the station manager just leading the group around.

Most college and university departments of radio-TV, film, speech and theatre, and journalism are in close touch with commercial broadcasters in their area. They frequently draw on stations for facilities, guest lecturers and part-time staff members. It's good to let your staff teach, if they wish. Not only is teaching a respectable way for a staff member to add a little to his or her income, it may provide an intellectual outlet not available within the day-to-day routine of the station.

And, again, a staff member is out rubbing elbows with members of the community, discovering the issues and ideas being discussed, and possibly important to your programming.

Stations frequently finance internship programs, in which outstanding students are subsidized while working as trainees. There are variations of this type of program. In major cities the structure of broadcast unions often prevents students from getting much professional experience, so the students often end up being observers more than doers. In New York City, one major professional group attempting to place interns has been frustrated by the complex union agreements, and by the stations and networks which have their own internal internship and minority training programs, and are not interested in taking on outside interns.

In contrast, in smaller and less structured markets, internships work to the mutual advantage of stations and educational institutions.

The stations get additional staff and the students get experience working under actual broadcast conditions. The schools end up with a pool of well-trained students with almost certain assurance they will be placed in a broadcasting job.

There are at least two basic arrangements. Some schools require that a student complete a professional internship before graduation. Frequently, these are set up as part-time jobs in local stations during the school term. Other schools go out and solicit scholarship-internships.

Here's the way an internship might work: A talented junior in a broadcast journalism program is selected to be an intern, starting at the beginning of the summer between the junior and senior years. Generally, the student works full time during the summer, and receives a weekly wage or stipend. When he or she returns in the fall, the station may provide scholarship assistance and employ the student parttime, or use the student as a campus news stringer.

A well thought out program should allow for a period of orientation, in which the student is taken on a thorough tour of the station and allowed to speak with various department heads. Then, a journalism student will frequently spend the balance of the summer working in the news department. A production student, however, may rotate through various departments to gain familiarity with each and, possibly, to fill in as vacation relief.

In any case, the student should have at least a brief opportunity to visit each department in the station and observe what goes on. The department head or supervisor should be instructed to set aside time to provide the intern with a detailed explanation of the department's duties and organization. It is important that the student intern understand the complete workings of a station, so that he or she will understand the interrelationship of all functions to the final product.

Our theoretical journalism student will probably start out in the newsroom as what is sometimes called a "desk assistant." The first duties assigned will probably amount to answering the telephone and tending to the loading and clearing (removing copy) of wire service teleprinters.

The student should be encouraged to try other skills, such as writing dry runs on scripts, shooting film or even air work. Since most students in this sort of program have a pretty solid foundation, they often advance quickly to take over the less skilled duties assigned to writers, photographers and reporters. Here again, a lot depends on union restrictions and the ability of the student. Sometimes a bright student from a school with a solid program finds himself filling in for other employees.

Any station management, which has long term concern for the broadcast industry, should be working closely with the schools, colleges and universities in the area to promote the training of able young people for the industry. The broadcast field needs a constant supply of creative people, who are trained in needed skills and precepts.

Obviously, the station benefits from being able to develop good entry-level employees, some of whom will stay and grow with the firm. Others, will go on to other markets, leaving you to recall the contribution you made to the industry by giving so and so, his or her start.

Having bright young people around acts as a stimulus to your staff. They ask questions—about systems, assumptions, methods, programs and rules which often cause you to rethink, just why you do certain things. Many a journalist, who was suddenly faced with cries for "advocacy journalism" in the late 1960s, had to stop and think out just why she or he was not and could not be an advocate. Out of the same period of questioning and turmoil came the conclusion, that the media did have a long way to go in reporting the problems and concerns of certain elements of our society.

Teaching and showing young people tends to stimulate your staff. Even the most challenging job becomes routine to a skilled practitioner, and it's often stimulating to have to teach someone else what you do—and explain why you do it.

A number of station managers praise internship programs, because they eventually provide stations with good solid "homegrown" staff, who know and belong to the community, and who lend stability to the station's overall operation.

SUMMARY

Being a good community citizen is an important role for every broadcasting station. It takes concern on the part of management, to make the time to participate; to spend the time to stimulate staff participation; and, occasionally, to spend a couple of dollars just for the good of the community. The effort can return dividends in audience, billing, news contacts, and at renewal time.

AWARDS

The following is a list of some of the awards given broadcasters each year, in recognition of the excellence of individual programs— or of overall programming.

We make no claim as to the list's completeness, although we believe it represents the majority of awards currently being given. The list is alphabetical by organization.

Action for Children's Television

Award—Achievement in Children's Television

Purpose—To encourage diversity and reduce commercialism on television programs for children.

Categories—Networks, Station Groups, Local Stations (more interested in trends than individual programs).

Contact—Action for Children's Television,
46 Austin Street
Newtonville, Massachusetts 02160,
Telephone: 617-527-7870.

Amalgamated Clothing and Textile Workers Union

Award—Sidney Hillman Foundation Awards

Purpose—To recognize outstanding achievements in mass communications.

Eligibility—All broadcast stations.

Deadline—Last day of January for preceding calendar year

Contact—Executive Director
Sidney Hillman Foundation
Amalgamated Clothing and Textile Workers Union
15 Union Square
New York, New York 10003
Telephone: 202-255-7800

American Bar Association

Award—Gavel Awards

Purpose—For outstanding contributions to public understanding of the American system of law and justice.

(1) Foster greater public understanding of the inherent values of our American legal and judicial system.

(2) Inform and educate citizens as to the roles of the law, the courts, law enforcement agencies, and the legal profession in today's society.

(3) Disclose practice and procedures in need of correction or improvement.

(4) Encourage and promote local, state and federal legislative efforts to update and modernize our nation's laws, courts and law enforcement agencies.

Eligibility—Documentary, educational and dramatic programs. Only five entries by any one organization. Entries may be related to current, historical or futuristic areas.

Categories—TV and Radio Networks, Network Owned and Operated TV and Radio Stations, TV and Radio Stations (three market size categories: Markets 1-10, 11-50, 51 and over); Educational and Public Broadcasting Radio and TV Stations; Cable.

Deadline—Material must have been broadcast during previous calendar year and postmarked not later than March 1 of current year.

Contact—American Bar Association, Committee on Gavel Awards, 1155 East 60th Street, Chicago, Illinois 60637; Telephone: 312-947-4161.

American Cancer Society

Award—Mass Media Awards Program (14 Awards)

Purpose—Honor best radio and TV programs dealing with the subject of cancer to educate the public.

Categories—Network Radio (spots and programs); Local Radio (spots, programs, continuing overall effort); Network TV (series, specials, personality, news and documentaries); Local TV (personality, specials, news and documentaries).

Deadline—October 1

Contact—American Cancer Society, Mass Media Awards Committee, 801 Second Avenue, New York, New York 10017, Telephone: 212-749-8038.

American Chiropractic Association

Award—The Health Journalism Award

Purpose—Honors meritorious programming in bringing public attention to the health needs of the nation.

Categories—Television: stories, features, programs; Radio: stories, features, programs.

Deadline—March 1 of current year for previous calendar year.

Contact—Journalism Awards, American Chiropractic Association, 2200 Grand Avenue, Des Moines, Iowa 50312, Telephone: 515-243-1121.

American Heart Association

Award—Howard W. Blakeslee Awards

Purpose—To encourage the attainment of the highest standards of reporting to the public on the heart and circulatory diseases.

Eligibility—Entries must have been broadcast on any recognized national or local medium of communication.

Deadline—Entries must have been broadcast in the U.S. or its territories during the period from March 1 to February 28. Entries must be submitted by midnight, May 1 following contest year.

Contact—Chairman, Managing Committee, Howard W. Blakeslee Awards, American Heart Association, 7320 Greenville Avenue, Dallas, Texas 75231, Telephone 214-750-5551.

Arthritis Foundation

Award—Cecil Award

Categories—Radio and Television

Deadline—Eligible materials must be broadcast in media generally available to the public between January 1 and December 13. Deadline is usually six weeks into following calendar year.

Contact—Senior Vice President
Administration and Operations
The Arthritis Foundation
3400 Peachtree Road NE Suite 1101
Atlanta, Georgia 30326
Telephone: 404-266-0795

American Legion

Award—American Legion Fourth Estate Award

Purpose—Recognition for activity or accomplishment which is national in scope or in its impact, and which contributed to the preservation of the American way of life.

Eligibility—Programming of national scope.

Categories—All Communications Media.

Deadline—15 days prior to annual spring meeting of National Executive Committee.

Contact—Director, National Public Relations Division, American Legion, 1608 K Street, NW, Washington, D.C. 20006, Telephone: 202-393-4811.

American Water Works Association

Award—American Water Works Association Communications Award

Purpose—Recognize the best coverage of the public drinking water supply story.

Deadline—January 1 for preceding calendar year

Contact—American Water Works Association
6666 West Quincy Avenue
Denver, Colorado 80235
Telephone: 303-892-9750 (call collect)

Associated Press Broadcasters Association

Award—Robert Eunson Award

Purpose—For distinguished service to broadcast journalism. No other information supplied.

Contact—Associated Press Broadcasters Association, c/o The Associated Press, 50 Rockefeller Plaza, New York, New York 10020, Telephone: 212-262-4000.

Note: The AP has state and regional awards. Contact the state or regional AP office for information.

Atlantic City, New Jersey

Award—National Headliner Award (13 Awards)

Purpose—Honors consistent, outstanding reporting; outstanding public service; outstanding documentaries.

Categories—Radio Stations (2 categories: cities over and under 250,000); Radio Networks; Television Stations (2 categories: cities over and under 500,000).

Deadline—Contact below.

Contact—Public Information Officer, Atlantic City, City Hall, Atlantic City, New Jersey, Telephone: 609-344-2121.

Aviation/Space Writers Association

Awards—James J. Strebig Memorial Award
Robert S. Ball Memorial Award
Earl D. Osborn Award
Public Information Officer Award
Harry Lever Award
Lauren D. Lyman Award
Distinguished Public Service Award

Purpose—To honor reporting and writing on space and aviation.

Eligibility—All space and aviation writers.

Categories—Television and Radio, Documentary.

Deadline—January 31 of current year for past calendar year.

Contact—Aviation/Space Writers Association, Secretary, Cliffwood Road, Chester, New Jersey 07930.

Broadcast Industry Conference

Award—Broadcast Preceptor Awards
Broadcast Media Awards
CATV Community Service Awards

Purpose—Honors outstanding contributions to the industry; excellence of local programming.

Eligibility—Nominations may come from a network, station or individual.

Categories—Broadcast Preceptors: Production and performance; Industry leadership; Academic leadership; Broadcast Media: Local programming, Local newscasts, Documentary, Special events, Editorial, Entertainment; CATV.

Deadline—March 1 of current year for preceding calendar year.

Contact—Conference Chairperson, Broadcast Industry Conference, San Francisco State University, 1600 Holoway Avenue, San Francisco, California 94132, Telephone: 415-469-2445.

Columbia University—School of Engineering and Applied Science

Award—Armstrong Award, sponsored by Armstrong Memorial Research Foundation.

Purpose—Honors excellence and originality in creating FM programs of the greatest benefit to the audience.

Eligibility—FM stations, commercial and non-commercial.

Categories—Music, Hard News, News Documentaries, Education, Public or Community Service, Creative Use of Media.

Deadline—February of current year for preceding year's programs.

Contact—Office Manager, Armstrong Awards Program, 510 Seeley W. Mudd Building, Columbia University, New York, New York 10027, Telephone: 212-280-4150.

Connecticut Business Journalism Awards

Award—Awards in Connecticut Business Journalism

Purpose—To encourage the highest possible standards of responsibility, clarity, accuracy, and insight in the writing and implementation of business news.

Eligibility—All entries must be about Connecticut business and industry. Entries are not limited to Connecticut media.

Deadline—Covers period January 1 to December 31. Entries must be postmarked no later than February 1.

Contact: Connecticut Business Journalism Awards
P.O. Box 3598
Hartford, Connecticut 06103

Corporation for Public Broadcasting Awards

Award—Corporation for Public Broadcasting Local Programming Awards

Purpose—Recognize outstanding local programs produced by local non-commercial radio and TV stations.

Eligibility—All public broadcast stations.

Deadline—Changes annually

Contact—Office of Public Affairs
1111 16th Street NW
Washington, D.C. 20036
Telephone: 202-293-6150

Economic News Broadcasters Association:

Award—Martin R. Gainsbrugh Award

Purpose—To honor excellence in economic news broadcasting

Categories—Radio, local; Radio—group station or network; Television, local; Television—group station or network.

Deadline—Last business day of Ocotober.

Contact—The Gainsbrugh Award
National Dividend Foundation
1000 East 17th Street
Riviera Beach, Florida 33404
Telephone: 305-845-6065

Education Writers Association

Award—Charles Stewart Mott Award

Purpose—To honor education writing.

Eligibility—Any broadcast media.

Categories—Single programs or series of reports on the same subject or theme, but not to exceed 60 minutes.

Deadline—Mid-February for preceding calendar year

Contact—Education Writers Association
P.O. Box 281
Woodstown, New Jersey 09098
Telephone: 609-769-1313

Freedoms Foundation

Award—George Washington Award

Purpose—Recognizes most outstanding individual contributions supporting human dignity and American credo.

Eligibility—U.S. citizens, companies, organizations, radio, TV, sponsors, educators.

Categories—Journalism, Editorials, Communication/Film, TV Programs, Radio Programs, Motion Picture, Governmental Activities.

Deadline—Covers period October 1 to October 1 or for academic year, October 1 through July 1. Chosen week following Thanksgiving and presented following Washington's Birthday.

Contact—Awards Administration, Freedoms Foundation at Valley Forge, Valley Forge, Pennsylvania 19481, Telephone: 215-433-8825.

George A. Grady School of Journalism—University of Georgia

Award—George Foster Peabody Award

Purpose—Recognizes public service.

Categories—Radio Documentary, Investigative Reporting, Viewer-Oriented Programming, Magazine Show, Contributions to Educational Television, Outstanding Musical Programming, Educational Programming, Historical Program.

Contact—Dean, George A. Grady School of Journalism
University of Georgia
Athens, Georgia 30602
Telephone: 404-542-1704

Information Film Producers of America

Award—Cindy Competition

Purpose—To honor outstanding films, videotapes, filmstrips and slide films.

Eligibility—Open to IFPA and non-IFPA members.

Categories—15 categories of films and videotapes including television information productions.

Deadline—June 15 for period June 1 of previous year to May 15 of current year

Contact—IFPA National Office
Attn: Cindy Competition
3518 Chuega Boulevard, West
Suite 313
Hollywood, California 90068
Telephone: 213-874-2266

Robert F. Kennedy Journalism Awards

Award—Same

Purpose—To recognize outstanding coverage of the problems of the disadvantaged.

Eligibility—Professional and Student Journalists (Separate contest for students who can win a three-month internship in Washington.)

Categories—Broadcast, Student

Deadline—January 28

Contact—Executive Director
Robert F. Kennedy Journalism Awards
1035 30th Street, NW
Washington, D.C. 20007
Telephone: 202-338-7444

Media Awards for the Advancement of Economic Understanding

Award—Same

Purpose—To give recognition to outstanding economic reporting directed to the general public. Patterned after the Pulitzer awards, the program is designed to stimulate media to initiate economic reporting that is imaginative, interesting and easily understandable.

Eligibility—Entries must be original works broadcast or telecast between January 1 and December 31.

Categories—A total of $105,000 is awarded in 14 media categories, competitively grouped according to circulation or scope of market. In each category there is a First Prize of $5,000 and a Second Prize of $2,500.

Deadline—January 15 of following year.

Contact—Program Administrator
Media Awards for the Advancement of Economic Understanding
Amos Tuck School of Business Administration
Dartmouth College
Hanover, New Hampshire 03755

Mortgage Bankers Association of America

Award—The Janus Awards

Purpose—For excellence in financial news programming. Recognizes commercial radio and TV stations and networks that produce financial and economic news programming that is comprehensive, informative, authoritative, interesting.

Categories—Radio Station, TV Station, Radio Network, TV Network.

Deadline—January 30 of current year for material broadcast during preceding calendar year.

Contact—Public Relations Department, Mortgage Bankers Association of America, 1125 15th Street NW, Washington, D.C. 20005, Telephone: 202-785-8333.

More Magazine

Award—A.J. Leibling Award

Purpose—Established in honor of A.J. Leibling the press critic
To honor journalism over a sustained period of time.

Eligible—Any working journalist including editorial drawings.

Deadline—Prior to Liebling convention—date changes annually.

Contact—Managing Editor

MORE Magazine

40 West 57th Street

New York, New York 10019

Telephone: 212-757-3040

National Academy of Television Arts and Sciences

Award—Emmy Awards

The National Award for Community Service

The Trustees Award

Purpose—To honor and recognize outstanding achievement in television.

Eligibility—Television broadcasters

Categories—News and Documentaries, Outstanding Drama Series, Outstanding Limited Series, Religious Categories, Outstanding Writing for Special Program, Sports Programming in Every Phase.

Deadline—Formal deadline not decided. For 1976-77, year ended March 1977.

Contact—The National Academy of Arts and Sciences, 291 South La Cienega Boulevard, Beverly Hills, California 90211, Telephone: 213-659-0990

National Association of Recycling Industries

Award—Annual NARI Media Awards.

Purpose—Recognize outstanding coverage of recycling and resource recovery in America.

Eligibility—Any electronic media.

Categories—Wire Services, Radio, Television.

Deadline—October 31 of each year for material broadcast the previous calendar year.

Contact—Media Awards, National Association of Recycling Industries, 330 Madison Avenue, New York, New York 10017, Telephone: 212-867-7330.

National Association of Science Writers

Award—Science in Society Journalism Award

Purpose—To encourage and reward interpreting, probing, and monitoring the performance of the scientific and medical community.

Eligibility—Straight science stories are *not* eligible.

Categories—Stories dealing with the Life Sciences; stories dealing with Physical Sciences.

Deadline—May 1 of current year for previous calendar year.

Contact—Administrative Secretary, National Association of Science Writers, Box H, Sea Cliff, New York 11579.

National Association of Television Program Executives

Award—Iris Awards

Purpose—To recognize excellence in programming.

Eligibility—All television stations.

Deadline—Mid-December for period December 1 of prior year to November 30 of current year.

Contact—National Association of Television Program Executives Awards Committee
Box 5272
Lancaster, Pennsylvania 17601
Telephone: 717-626-4424

National Broadcast Editorial Association

Award—NBEA Awards

Purpose—To recognize excellence in radio and television editorials.

Eligibility—Awards will sample each of 12 months of station's editorials "to measure station's commitments to editorializing."

Deadline—March 1 for previous calendar year.

Contact—Philip Scribner Balboni, WCVB-TV, 5 TV Place, Needham, Massachusetts 02192, Telephone: 617-449-0400.

National Conference of Christians and Jews

Award—Brotherhood Awards

Purpose—Fostering of brotherhood and better understanding among people.

Eligibility—Any radio or TV station or network.

Categories—Editorial, Motion Picture, TV and Radio Programming (Network and Local), Documentaries, Interview Shows.

Deadline—End of year for same year.

Contact—Vice President and Director of Public Relations, The National Conference of Christians and Jews, 43 West 57th Street, New York, New York 10019, Telephone: 212-MU 8-7530.

National Press Club

Award—Fourth Estate Awards
   National Press Club Awards for Excellence in Consumer Reporting
Purpose—To take note of impact on a community and service performed.
Eligibility—Any news person who receives no less than 50 percent of income from such work. Only works aired during the previous year, up to award date.
Categories—TV Stations and Networks, Radio Stations and Networks, Wire Services, Consumer Reporting.
Deadline—Last day of May for previous 12 months.
Contact—Awards Committee, National Press Club, National Press Building, Washington, D.C. 20045, Telephone: 202-737-2500.

National Press Photographers Association

Awards—The Joseph A. Sprague Memorial Award
   The Joseph Costa Award
   NPPA Fellowship Award
   Kenneth P. McLaughlin Award of Merit
   Newsfilm Cameraman of the Year
   Newsfilm Station of the Year
Purpose—(1.) Honor achievement in photo journalism; (2). For most outstanding initiative, leadership and service in advancing NPPA goals; (3). Continuing outstanding service or technical achievement in photography; (4). Outstanding service.
Categories—To working and non-working press photographers.
Contact—President, National Press Photographers Association Attention: Jerry Gay, *The Seattle Times,* P.O. Box 70, Seattle, Washington 98111.

Overseas Press Club of America

Award—Madeline Dane Ross Award
   Bob Considine Memorial Award

Categories—Best radio spot news from abroad; Best radio interpretation of foreign news; Best TV spot news from abroad; Best TV interpretation or documentary on foreign affairs; Best business news reporting from abroad; For international reporting in any medium which demonstrates a concern for humanity; Best reporting from abroad requiring exceptional courage and iniative.

Deadline—February 11 of current year for preceding calendar year.

Contact—Awards Committee Chairman, Overseas Press Club, 55 East 43d Street, Hotel Biltmore, New York, New York 10017, Telephone: 212-687-2430.

Ohio State University Telecommunications Center

Award—The Ohio State Awards (sponsored by Institute for Education by Radio and Television)

Purpose—To recognize meritorious achievement in educational, informational and public affairs broadcasting.

Eligibility—Broadcasts from preceding academic year (September to August) must have been primarily designed to educate and must have been in English.

Categories—Performing Arts and Humanities; Natural and Physical Sciences; Social Sciences (Community Problems); Social Sciences (Individuals).

Deadline—August 15 for award given in following calendar year.

Contact—The Ohio State Awards, 2400 Olentangy River Road, Columbus, Ohio 43210, Telephone: 614-422-9678.

Radio-Television News Directors Association

Award—Edward R. Murrow Awards
   RTNDA Awards

Purpose—To recognize outstanding enterprise and social awareness in the reporting of significant community problems or issues, in whatever form.

Categories—Radio: Interpretive and Investigative Reporting.
   TV: Documentary, Interpretive, Investigative, In Depth Reporting of On-The-Spot News Story: Radio or TV; Investigative Reporting: Radio or TV; Editorial Awards: Radio or TV.

Deadline—March 1 of current year for preceding calendar year.

Contact—Chairman, Awards Committee, c/o Radio-Television News Directors Association, 1735 DeSales Street, NW, Washington, D.C. 20036, Telephone: 202-737-8657.

RTNDA also has a regional awards program.

Religion In Media

Award—R.I.M. AWARDS PROGRAM

Purpose—Honor those who have contributed to the presentation of moral and spiritual values through the entertainment media

Categories—Radio, Television, Journalism, Special Media

Deadline—December 31 of current year

Contact—R.I.M. Awards Coordinator
Religion in Media Association
1776 N. Gower Street
Hollywood, California 90028
Telephone: 213-466-3342

Society of Professional Journalists—Sigma Delta Chi

Award—Sigma Delta Chi Awards for Distinguished Service in Journalism

Purpose—To honor distinguished service in journalism.

Categories—Radio reporting; Public Service in radio journalism; Editorializing on Radio; Television Reporting; Public Service in Television Journalism; Editorializing on Television; Research in Journalism.

Deadline—January 25 of current year for preceding calendar year.

Contact—Sigma Delta Chi Awards, Society of Professional Journalists—Sigma Delta Chi, 35 East Wacker Drive, Suite 3108, Chicago, Illinois 60601, Telephone: 312-236-6577.

Note: Many of the local affiliates of SPJ-SDX have their own awards programs serving their regions.

Scripps-Howard Foundation

Award—Roy W. Howard Public Service Award

Purpose —To recognize TV and radio stations for outstanding public service—that is, the exposure of and alleviation of corruption, crime, health or other problems inimical to the general welfare.

Eligibility—Open to any TV or radio station in the U.S. and its territories.

Deadline—March 1 of current year for preceding calendar year.

Contact—Roy W. Howard Awards, The Scripps-Howard Foundation, 500 Central Avenue, Cincinnati, Ohio 45202, Telephone: 513-621-0130.

Southern Baptist Radio and TV Commission

Award—Abe Lincoln Awards to Distinguished Broadcasters
Abe Lincoln Railsplitter

Purpose—To honor achievements in advancing the quality of life in America and for helping the broadcast industry enrich its service to the public; Railsplitter Award—for serving community, station and industry through pioneering efforts.

Eligibility—All broadcasters.

Categories—Commercial and Educational Radio and TV: Management, Programming, Promotion, Public Service, News and Public Affairs, other. By market categories: (under 50,000, 50,000–100,00, 100,000–500,000, 500,000-up).

Deadline—September 1 for year ending preceding June 30.

Contact—Southern Baptist Radio and TV Commission, 6350 West Freeway, Fort Worth, Texas 76116, Telephone: 817-737-4011.

United Press International

UPI gives no national awards, but there is a program of state and regional awards recognizing superior broadcast efforts. Information can be obtained through state and regional UPI offices.

UNDA U.S.A.

Award—Gabriel Awards

Purpose—To honor excellence in broadcasting: both programs and individuals.

Categories—Entertainment; Information-Education; Religious; Youth-Oriented; Personal Achievement; Station Award.

Deadline—September 15 for period from July 1 of previous year to June 30 of current year

Contact—Gabriel Awards Chairperson, UNDA—U.S.A. Catholic Radio-TV Center, 1027 Superior Ave., Room 630, Cleveland, Ohio 44114, Telephone: 216-579-1633.

Writers Guild of America

Award—WGA Writing Awards

Purpose—To honor writers specifically, according to the judgment of their peers.

Categories—Radio-TV Documentary Script; TV-Documentary; Current Events.

Deadline—January of current year for preceding calendar year.

Contact—Awards Coordinator, Writers Guild of America, 22 West 48th Street, New York, New York 10036, Telephone: 212-575-5060.

Women in Communications, Incorporated

Award—Clarion Awards

Purpose—For outstanding communication in the areas of human rights, resources and the community.

Categories—Radio series or documentary, Television series or documentary.

Deadline—February 15 for preceding calendar year.

Contact—Clarion Awards, Women in Communications, Inc., P.O. Box 9561, Austin, Texas 78766.

Index

Index

251